CHEMISTRY 11

STUDY GUIDE

SENIOR PROGRAM CONSULTANT

Maurice DiGiuseppe, Ph.D.
University of Ontario Institute of Technology (UOIT)
Formerly of Toronto Catholic District School Board

NELSON / EDUCATION

NELSON EDUCATION

Nelson Chemistry 11 Study Guide

Senior Program Consultant
Maurice DiGiuseppe

Student Book Authors
Stephen Haberer
Kristina Salciccioli
Milan Sanader

Editorial Director
Linda Allison

Acting Publisher, Science
David Spiegel

Managing Editor, Development
Jennifer Hounsell

Product Manager
Lorraine Lue

Program Manager
Carmen Yu

Developmental Editor
Barbara Booth

Editorial Assistants
Michelle Irvine
Mina Shin

Copyeditor
Linda Szostak

Design Director
Ken Phipps

Interior Design
Courtney Hellam

Cover Design
Eugene Lo
Ken Phipps

Cover Image
Dorling Kindersley/Getty Images

Asset Coordinator
Suzanne Peden

Illustrators
Crowle Art Group
Steven Hall
Samuel Laterza
Dave McKay
Allan Moon
Suzanne Peden
PreMediaGlobal
Ann Sanderson

Compositor
PreMediaGlobal

Cover Research
Debbie Yea

Printer
Transcontinental Printing, Ltd.

Reviewers
The authors and publisher gratefully
acknowledge the contributions of
the following educators:
Charles J. Cohen
Mark Kinoshita
Richard LaChapelle
Anne Patrick
Steve Pfisterer

Contents

Unit 4 Solutions and Solubility. . . 129

Unit 5 Gases and Atmospheric Chemistry. 172

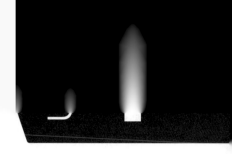

Chapter 1: Atomic Structure and the Periodic Table

Chemistry is the study of matter and its interactions. Understanding matter at its most fundamental level requires the understanding of the atom, the smallest unit of any pure element. The history of the atom stretches back more than 2000 years, progressing through a variety of advances made by scientists such as Dalton, Thomson, Rutherford, and Bohr. At the end of the process, the Bohr–Rutherford model of the atom emerged, showing that electrons orbit around the nucleus. In addition, the periodic table was developed as a way to systematically categorize elements and the atoms they are made up of. The periodic table arranges elements by atomic number (number of protons and electrons) and atomic mass. Trends in the periodic table run both horizontally left to right (atomic radius, electron affinity, first ionization energy), and up to down (effective nuclear charge).

Chapter 2: Chemical Compounds and Bonding

Compounds exist in two basic forms, ionic and molecular. Ionic compounds share similar properties. They are hard, brittle, crystalline solids with high melting and boiling points, high solubility in water, and high electrical conductance when dissolved. Molecular compounds are more variable, existing as solids, liquids, and gases at room temperature, often with low boiling and melting points, limited solubility, and limited ability to conduct electricity. Ionic compounds are held together by the electrostatic force between positive and negative ions in strong, non-sharing, ionic bonds. These rigid bonds give ionic compounds many of their properties, making them hard, brittle, and subject to ionization when exposed to highly polar water molecules. Molecular compounds get their character from their covalent bonds in which electrons can be equally shared (non-polar) or asymmetrically shared (polar covalent). Bond character is dependent on electronegativity differences between atoms.

Chapter 3: Molecular Compounds and Intermolecular Forces

Molecular compounds can exist in two basic forms: polar molecules and non-polar molecules. Two factors distinguish between the two types of molecular compound: the type of bonds that exist in the molecule and the molecule's shape. Water and carbon dioxide, for example, both seem to feature very similar configurations—three atoms and two polar covalent bonds. However, carbon dioxide is a non-polar compound, while water is highly polar. The difference between the two molecules is their shapes. Carbon dioxide's symmetrical shape cancels out charges, while water's bent shape accentuates polarity. The result is that water is a polar molecule with partially charged ends that can form hydrogen bonds between molecules. Hydrogen bonds are an example of the strongest type of intermolecular force that holds molecular compounds together. The other intermolecular forces are the dipole-dipole force (hydrogen bonds are actually a special type of dipole-dipole force) and London dispersion forces. Hydrogen bonds in water promote several unique properties, including low density of ice, high melting point, boiling point, surface tension, and heat capacity. All life on Earth is highly dependent on these properties of water.

BIG IDEAS

- Every element has predictable chemical and physical properties determined by its structure.

- The type of chemical bond in a compound determines the physical and chemical properties of that compound.

- It is important to use chemicals properly to minimize the risks to human health and the environment.

The Nature of Chemistry

Vocabulary

matter   empirical knowledge   theoretical knowledge   theory

LEARNING TIP

Conceptualizing in Chemistry
Understanding concepts in chemistry often requires trying to visualize things that we cannot see. There are many ways you can help yourself to be better at this. Try using hands-on manipulative models, working with computer simulations, or drawing images on paper.

MAIN IDEA: Chemistry is the study of matter and how it behaves in macroscopic and microscopic ways.

1. Matter is any substance that has _____ and _____. K/U

2. Fill in **Table 1**, summarizing what chemists do. K/U

Table 1 What Chemists Do

What chemists do	Macroscopic or microscopic	Type of knowledge gained	Where it occurs: in the lab or on paper
experiment			
conceptualize			
measure			
imagine			
theorize			
observe			

3. A chemist determines that a substance has a melting temperature of –8 °C. What kind of knowledge has the chemist gained? K/U
   (a) empirical knowledge
   (b) conceptual knowledge
   (c) theoretical knowledge
   (d) technological knowledge

4. For each of the items in **Table 2**, determine whether the item is a form of matter. Then explain how you know. C A

Table 2 Matter

Item	Is it matter? (yes/no)	How do you know?
wood		
air		
sleep		
gravity		

5. Complete the bubble map (**Figure 1**) to identify the characteristics of a theory. K/U

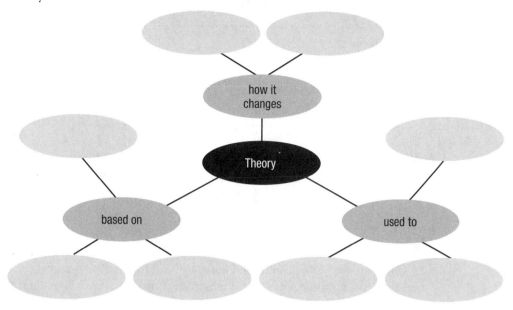

Figure 1

6. A scientist has five objects that are each about the size of an apple. She cannot see each object or feel its shape. All she can do is cause each object to roll on a smooth, flat, floor and observe its starting point and end point. Use the information given in **Table 3** to form a theory about each object. State your theory and sketch each object. C A

Table 3 Objects

Observation	Theory	Sketch
The object travels very slowly in a straight line.		
The object travels very fast in a straight line.		
The object travels smoothly, but it does not travel in a straight line.		
The object slides rather than rolls.		
The object travels in an erratic path and bounces up and down as it travels.		

Atomic Structure

Textbook pp. 11–16

Vocabulary			
atom	neutron	valence electron	mass number (*A*)
electron	energy level	atomic number (*Z*)	atomic mass unit
proton	valence shell		

MAIN IDEA: Atoms are the smallest particles that make up an element.

1. Rather than try to understand the nature of matter, most alchemists were searching for such things as the philosopher's stone, which had what property? K/U

2. Complete the Venn diagram in **Figure 1** to compare the atom models of Democritus, Dalton, and Bohr–Rutherford. Three items have been entered for you. K/U C

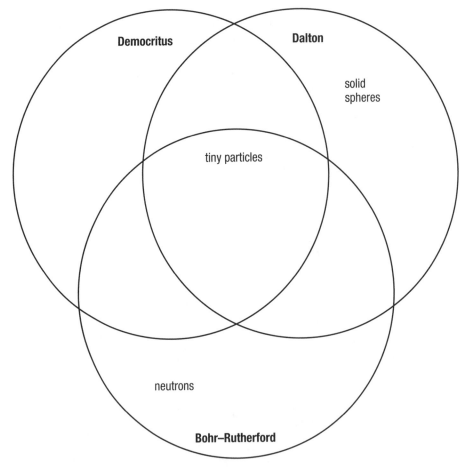

Democritus   Dalton

solid spheres

tiny particles

neutrons

Bohr–Rutherford

Figure 1

MAIN IDEA: Key experiments and ideas from Chadwick, Thomson, Rutherford, and Bohr helped chemists of today formulate a model of the atom.

LEARNING TIP

Le Système international d'unités
SI units, or le Système international d'unités, is a set of rules used around the world for scientific communication. The rules specify which units are used for which quantities. Appendix B1 lists many of the SI units commonly used in chemistry.

3. Rutherford's gold foil experiment fired positive alpha particles at a thin sheet of gold foil. K/U

   (a) What did Rutherford expect would happen to the particles?

   (b) What model was Rutherford using to make his assumption? Describe the model.

   (c) What result did Rutherford get and why did this result surprise him?

   (d) How did the result cause Rutherford to change his model of the atom?

4. Use **Table 1** to calculate your answers to the problems below. T/I

   Table 1 Subatomic particles

Subatomic particle	Symbol	Location in the atom	Change	Approximate mass (kg)
electron	e^-	in energy levels outside the nucleus	-1	9.11×10^{-31}
proton	p^+	in the nucleus	$+1$	1.67×10^{-27}
neutron	n^0	in the nucleus	0	1.67×10^{-27}

   (a) Which is greater in mass—a proton or an electron? How many times as great?

LEARNING TIP

Grass
Problem solving is better when you use the GRASS system. In this system, you start with G, the "Given," the data you start with. You then state your goal, R, for "Required." This is followed by A for "Analysis" and S for the "Solution" that your analysis produces. Finally, the last S stands for "Statement," a sentence that tells what you solved.

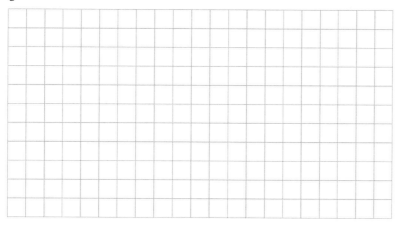

(b) The alpha particles used in the Rutherford gold foil experiment consisted of two protons and two neutrons. How did an alpha particle compare in size to an electron?

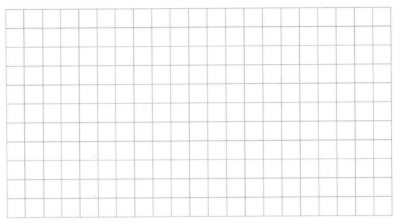

(c) How does your answer to part (b) support Rutherford's original expectation for the gold foil experiment? Explain.

(d) How does your answer to part (b) support the conclusion Rutherford drew from the gold foil experiment about the nucleus of an atom? Explain.

MAIN IDEA: You can determine the number of protons, neutrons, and electrons of an atom, and its mass number from the way it is expressed.

5. Determine the number of protons, neutrons, and electrons for each of the following hypothetical atoms. K/U T/I

   (a) $^{14}_{8}Xx$

   (b) $^{31}_{16}Gx$

   (c) $^{63}_{45}Rp$

6. A hypothetical element has a mass number of 14. T/I C

   (a) Write two different possible configurations for the element. List the number of protons, neutrons, and electrons that it has in each example.

   (b) Draw and label a model of one of the atoms you listed in part (a) above. Show each proton, neutron, and electron in your model.

Ions and the Octet Rule

Vocabulary			
full or stable octet	ion	valence	multivalent
octet rule	cation	anion	polyatomic ion

Textbook pp. 17–22

MAIN IDEA: The most stable configuration of an atom among the first 18 elements is to have its outer valence shell filled.

1. Among the first 18 elements, the most stable configuration for an atom is to have its outermost electron shell contain either _____ electrons or _____ electrons. K/U

2. Which of the following entities would be the most stable of one of the first 18 elements of the periodic table? K/U
   (a) an entity with 8 electrons
   (b) an entity with only 1 electron in its outer valence shell
   (c) an entity with a full inner shell
   (d) an entity with 8 electrons in its outer valence shell

3. Is the following statement true or false? If you think the statement is false, rewrite it to make it true: All of the noble gases among the first 18 elements are stable because they have 8 electrons in their valence shell. K/U

4. (a) Make a Bohr–Rutherford diagram of the following elements.
   (i) argon (atomic number: 18)
   (ii) sodium (atomic number: 11)
   (iii) phosphorus (atomic number: 15)

> **STUDY TIP**
>
> **Bohr–Rutherford Diagrams**
> When analyzing Bohr–Rutherford diagrams, always count electrons one shell at a time, starting with the innermost shell with only 2 electrons.

(i)	(ii)	(iii)

   (b) Which element from part (a) is the most stable? How do you know?

   (c) Which element is likely to gain electrons to become more stable? How many electrons is it likely to gain? How do you know?

   (d) Which element is likely to lose electrons to become more stable? How many electrons is it likely to lose? How do you know? K/U T/I

5. (a) Draw a diagram of a magnesium atom, Mg. Identify the valence electrons on your drawing.

   (b) Draw a diagram-equation to show what happens when Mg ionizes. Then use the information in your diagram-equation to fill in **Table 1** and **Table 2**.

Table 1 Magnesium Atom

# of protons	
# of neutrons	
# of electrons	
charge	

Table 2 Magnesium Ion

# of protons	
# of neutrons	
# of electrons	
charge	

   (c) What charge does Mg take when it ionizes?

   (d) Why is Mg more stable after it ionizes? What noble gas does the Mg ion resemble? K/U T/I

6. (a) Draw a diagram-equation to show what happens when sulfur ionizes. Fill in **Table 3** and **Table 4**.

Table 3 Sulfur Atom

# of protons	
# of neutrons	
# of electrons	
charge	

Table 4 Sulfur Ion

# of protons	
# of neutrons	
# of electrons	
charge	

   (b) What is the name of the ion you created? _____

   (c) Why is sulfur more stable after it ionizes? What noble gas does the sulfur ion resemble? K/U

MAIN IDEA: Ions can be multivalent. To make sure there is no confusion, always use the IUPAC system to name ions and compounds.

7. Write the classical and IUPAC name for each ion. K/U

    (a) Cu^{2+}

    (b) Cl^-

    (c) Pb^{2+}

    (d) SO_3^{2-}

8. A compound of tin, Sn, and fluoride, F^-, is used in toothpastes. One tin(II) ion combines with two F^- ions. The name of this compound is _____ fluoride. K/U

9. A compound of iron, Fe, and oxygen, O, forms rust. Two iron(III) ions combine with three O^{2-} ions. The name of this compound is _____. K/U

Isotopes, Radioisotopes, and Atomic Mass

Textbook pp. 23–29

Vocabulary

isotope	radioactive decay	beta particle	radioactive
isotopic abundance	nuclear radiation	gamma ray	atomic mass
mass spectrometer	alpha particle	radioisotope	

MAIN IDEA: Most elements have different isotopes that vary in atomic mass.

1. Two different isotopes of an element have the same number of
   _____ but different numbers of _____. K/U

2. Is the following statement true or false? If you think the statement is false, rewrite it to make it true: The atomic mass of the element magnesium is not a whole number, but all isotopes of magnesium have a whole number of protons and neutrons. K/U

3. Diagrams of four isotopes are shown in **Figure 1**. K/U T/I

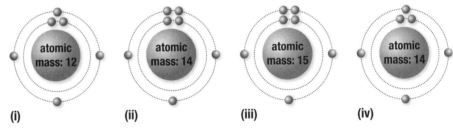

(i)   (ii)   (iii)   (iv)

Figure 1

(a) Which diagram, if any, identifies the same element as diagram (i)? How do you know?

(b) Which diagram, if any, identifies the same element as diagram (ii)? How do you know?

(c) Diagram (i) represents which isotope of what element? _____

(d) Diagram (ii) represents which isotope of what element? _____

(e) Diagram (iii) represents which isotope of what element? _____

(f) Diagram (iv) represents which isotope of what element? _____

4. (a) Draw and label diagrams to represent two isotopes of oxygen, including the most common isotope.

(b) Which diagram represents the most abundant oxygen isotope in nature? How do you know?

(c) How abundant would you expect your second isotope to be in nature? Explain. K/U C A

5. **Figure 2** shows a mass spectrometer that has a sample of boron ions being accelerated into the detector screen. T/I

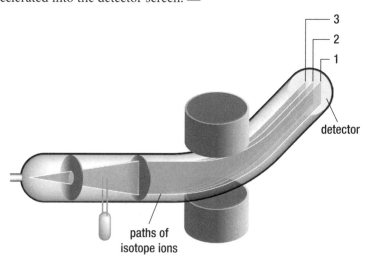

Figure 2

(a) Which ion path identifies the lightest isotope of boron? The heaviest? How do you know?

(b) Fill in **Table 1** using the information in **Figure 2**.

Table 1 Boron Isotopes

Boron isotope	Path	Protons	Neutrons
B-10			
B-11			
B-12			

1.4 Isotopes, Radioisotopes, and Atomic Mass

6. A form of nuclear radiation has the following characteristics:
   - It is blocked by a lead sheet.
   - It is a charged particle.
   - Its mass is less than the mass of a hydrogen atom.

   What kind of radiation is it? Explain how you know. C A

7. You have a substance that you suspect is a radioisotope. What characteristics would you expect this substance to have? K/U

LEARNING **TIP**

Working with Weighted Averages
Whether you realize it or not, you work with weighted averages all the time. Your final mark in a course is usually determined by calculating a weighted average of your semester work (70 %) and your final summative assessment and/or culminating activity (30 %).

8. Use the isotopic composition data below to calculate the atomic mass of zinc. T/I
   Zn-64: 48.6 %
   Zn-66: 27.9 %
   Zn-67: 4.10 %
   Zn-68: 18.8 %
   Zn-70: 0.60 %

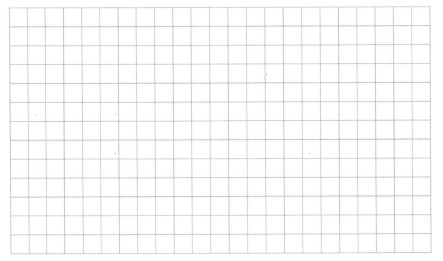

The Periodic Table and Periodic Law

Textbook pp. 30–33

Vocabulary

metalloid   period   periodic law   Lewis symbol

group

MAIN IDEA: The periodic table is arranged to show patterns of characteristics of the elements.

1. Vertical columns called _____ feature atoms that all share the same number of _____. K/U

2. Is the following statement true or false? If you think the statement is false, rewrite it to make it true: All elements within a period or row of the periodic table share similar properties of reactivity. K/U

3. Where are the most reactive elements located in the periodic table? K/U
    (a) in Groups 1 and 17
    (b) in Group 18
    (c) in Groups 3–12
    (d) in Periods 6 and 7

4. Fill in **Table 1** to identify the properties and characteristics of different families and groups of the periodic table. K/U

Table 1 Properties of Elements

Group	Location	Reactivity	Metal or non-metal?	State at room temperature	Reacts with
halogens					
alkali metals					
noble gases					
transition metals					
alkaline earth metals					

5. What patterns can you identify within a typical period in the periodic table? Describe a typical pattern. Be sure you name the groups involved. K/U

6. How does the valence of atoms change: K/U
   (a) within a group?

   (b) within a period?

7. Draw Lewis symbol diagrams for the elements listed below. Fill in **Table 2** to explain how the Lewis diagram predicts reactivity for each element. K/U C

Table 2 Lewis Diagram Reactivity Prediction

Element	Explanation	Lewis diagram
P		
Kr		
Li		
Al		

8. Mystery element X has the properties listed below. Identify element X. Explain how you identified the element. T/I
   - Element X is a representative element.
   - Element X reacts strongly with oxygen, and less strongly with water.
   - Element X is a light, solid metal.
   - Element X is bordered on one side by a transition metal.
   - Element X is not strontium.

A Not-So-Elementary Task

Textbook pp. 34–35

MAIN IDEA: The periodic table was a collaborative effort that took centuries to complete.

1. The first scientist to discover a repeating pattern among the elements was
_____. K/U

2. Is the following statement true or false? If you think the statement is false, rewrite it to make it true: Before Hennig Brand discovered phosphorous in urine, no elements were known. K/U

3. Which of the following identifies the key insight that Mendeleev used to organize his table? K/U
   (a) organizing elements by their reactivity
   (b) organizing elements by valence
   (c) organizing elements by their atomic mass
   (d) organizing elements by the number of neutrons they had

4. Complete **Table 1** to summarize the development of the Periodic Table. K/U

Table 1 Development of the Periodic Table

Scientist	Date	Scheme	Strength	Flaw
Brand	1649	isolated first element	began search for elements	no pattern found
Lavoisier	1789			
Dobereiner	1800s			
Newlands	1649			
Mendeleev	1869			
Lothar Meyer	1864			
Moseley	1900s			
Seaborg	1940s			

5. Look at the first 18 elements of the periodic table. Subtract the atomic number of each element from the atomic number of the element below it. What pattern do you see? Does this pattern continue on lower rows of the table? T/I

Periodic Trends in Atomic Properties

Textbook pp. 36–41

Vocabulary

atomic radius   ionic radius   ionization energy   electron affinity

effective nuclear charge

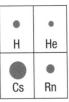
MAIN IDEA: The atomic radii of atoms change in a predictable pattern that corresponds to periods in the periodic table.

1. Which trend applies to all atoms in the periodic table? K/U

   (a) Atomic radius increases as the atomic number increases.
   (b) Atomic radius decreases as the atomic number increases within a single period.
   (c) Atomic radius decreases as the atomic number increases within a single group.
   (d) Atomic radius increases as the atomic number increases within a single period and within a single group.

2. Which trend applies to all atoms in the periodic table? K/U

   (a) Within a period, shielding increases as the atomic number increases.
   (b) Within a period, effective nuclear charge decreases as the atomic number increases.
   (c) Within a group, shielding increases as the atomic number increases.
   (d) Within a group, effective nuclear charge increases as the atomic number increases.

3. In a diatomic oxygen molecule, the atomic radius is defined as _____ the distance between the centres of the _____ of the two oxygen atoms. K/U

4. Compare the atoms, nitrogen, N, oxygen, O, and sulfur, S, in **Figure 1.** K/U

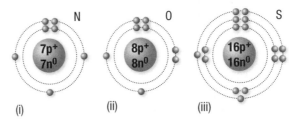

Figure 1

   (a) Between oxygen and nitrogen, which atom has a greater effective nuclear charge? How do you know?

(b) With respect to atomic radius, what is the consequence of your answer to part (a)? Explain.

(c) Between oxygen and sulfur, which atom has a greater effective nuclear charge? How do you know?

(d) With respect to atomic radius, what is the consequence of your answer to part (c)? Explain.

MAIN IDEA: The ionic radius of atoms change in a predictable pattern that corresponds to periods in the periodic table.

5. (a) Draw the sodium ion that results when sodium is ionized in **Figure 2**.

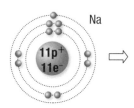

Figure 2 Ionization of a sodium atom

(b) In the Na atom, what fraction of the total nuclear attraction force does each electron have?

(c) In the Na ion, what fraction of the total nuclear attraction force does each electron have?

(d) Which is greater—the force on each electron in the sodium atom or in the sodium ion? How does this affect the size of each entity? T/I C

6. (a) Draw the chlorine ion that results when chlorine is ionized in **Figure 3**.

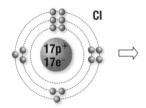

Figure 3 Ionization of a chlorine atom

(b) In the Cl atom, what fraction of the total nuclear attraction force does each electron have? In the Cl ion, what fraction of the total nuclear attraction force does each electron have?

(c) Which is greater—the force on each electron in the chlorine atom or in the chlorine ion? How does this affect the size of each entity? How does chlorine's hold compare to that of sodium in Question 5? T/I A

MAIN IDEA: The ionization energy and electron affinity of atoms change in a predictable pattern that corresponds to periods in the periodic table.

7. When a chlorine atom gets ionized, energy is _____. K/U

8. Which trends apply with respect to atomic radius, electronegativity, and electron affinity in the periodic table? K/U

(a) From left to right: atomic radius ↓ electro-negativity ↑ electron affinity ↑

(b) From left to right: atomic radius ↑ electro-negativity ↑ electron affinity ↑

(c) From left to right: atomic radius ↑ electro-negativity ↓ electron affinity ↑

(d) From left to right: atomic radius ↓ electro-negativity ↑ electron affinity ↓

Atomic Structure and the Periodic Table

The graphic organizer below summarizes some of the main ideas from Chapter 1.
Add your own notes to the graphic organizer to create study notes.

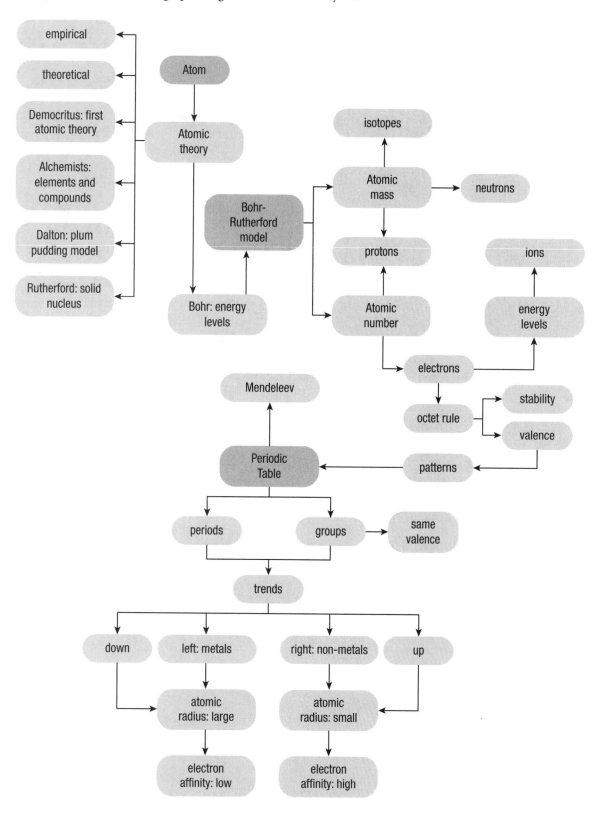

K/U Knowledge/Understanding
T/I Thinking/Investigation
C Communication
A Application

1. Identify each kind of knowledge that is involved in baking a loaf of bread as either theoretical or empirical. (1.1) K/U A
   (a) Finding out that bread rises best when mixed in water about 40 °C. _____
   (b) Finding out that bread fails to rise in water above 60 °C. _____
   (c) Stating that the ideal temperature for rising might be midway between 40 °C and 60 °C. _____
   (d) Stating that the yeast that cause bread to rise live well in warm water but get killed off in hot water. _____

2. Which of the following conclusions did Rutherford's gold foil experiment lead to? (1.2) K/U
   (a) Atoms are incredibly small.
   (b) Atoms are mostly empty space.
   (c) Electrons exist only in discrete energy levels.
   (d) Protons are positively charged and electrons are negatively charged.

3. Is the following statement true or false? If you think the statement is false, rewrite it to make it true: The "holes" in Mendeleev's periodic table proved that some elements did not fit into his scheme. (1.6) K/U

4. A lithium atom has 3 protons and 4 neutrons. (1.2) T/I
   (a) What is the mass of a lithium atom in u? _____
   (b) What is the mass of a lithium atom in kg? _____

5. Fill in **Table 1** to compare ions and atoms. K/U

Table 1 Ions and Atoms

	Proton	Neutron	Electron
atom			
negative ion			
positive ion			

6. (a) Complete **Figure 1** to show how a potassium atom ionizes. Then write the equation below.

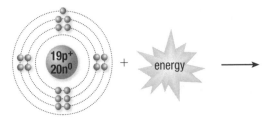

Figure 1

(b) Fill in **Table 2** and **Table 3**. (1.3) ▣ ▣

Table 2 Potassium Atom

# of protons	
# of neutrons	
# of electrons	
charge	

Table 3 Potassium Ion

# of protons	
# of neutrons	
# of electrons	
charge	

7. Calcium has an atomic mass of 40.078 u with 20 protons and 20 electrons. (1.4) ▣

   (a) What is likely to be the most common calcium isotope in terms of protons, neutrons, and electrons?

   (b) What other calcium isotope might you find in terms of protons, neutrons, and electrons? How abundant would this isotope likely be? Explain.

8. The Lewis symbol for unknown element X is shown in **Figure 2**. X has more than 20 neutrons, but its atomic mass is less than 100 u. Which element is X? (1.5) ▣ ▣ _____

Figure 2

9. (a) Fill in **Table 4** to compare bromine, Br, to potassium, K. (1.7)

Table 4 Bromine and Potassium Comparison

	Bromine (Br)	**Potassium (K)**
number of protons		
atomic radius		
ionic radius		
electron affinity		
number of valence electrons		
screening of the nucleus		
first ionization energy		

(b) Explain the difference in first ionization energy in the above table. ▣ ▣

Ionic Compounds

Textbook pp. 56-60

> **Vocabulary**
>
> chemical bond   ionic bond   formula unit   ionic compound
>
> electrolyte

MAIN IDEA: The properties of ionic compounds are distinctive and can be predicted by the nature of the ionic bonds that hold them together.

1. An ionic compound combines a _____ and a _____ joined together by an ionic bond. K/U

2. A(n) _____ force holds the positive and negative ions in an ionic bond together. K/U

3. A substance seems to have all of the characteristics of an ionic compound except one. When dissolved in water, this solid fails to conduct electricity. Can the substance be an ionic compound? K/U T/I

    (a) No, all dissolved ionic compounds are good conductors of electricity, so the substance cannot be an ionic compound.

    (b) No, most ionic compounds can conduct electricity only in the solid state, so the substance is not likely to be an ionic compound.

    (c) Yes, most but not all dissolved ionic compounds are good conductors of electricity, so this substance must be one of the few ionic compounds that is not a good conductor.

    (d) Yes, ionic compounds conduct electricity only when they exist in a liquid state, so when dissolved in water, you would not expect the compound to be a conductor.

4. Is the following statement true or false? If you think the statement is false, rewrite it to make it true: Any sample of water that is a good conductor of electricity must have some electrolytes dissolved in it. K/U

5. Draw Lewis symbols to show the formation of the following compounds. K/U C

    (a) potassium bromide

    (b) calcium chloride

6. Explain why there is no such thing as a single molecule of sodium chloride. A

7. Complete **Figure 1** to summarize the properties of ionic compounds. K/U C

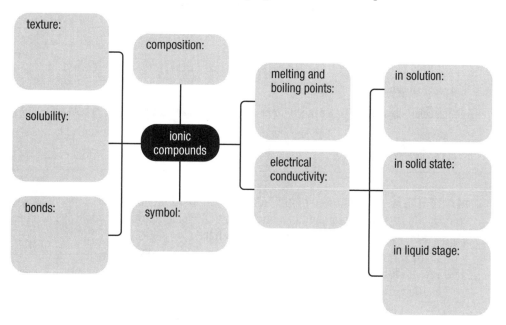

texture:

composition:

solubility:

ionic compounds

melting and boiling points:

in solution:

electrical conductivity:

in solid state:

bonds:

symbol:

in liquid stage:

Figure 1

8. Complete **Table 1** to explain the properties of ionic compounds. K/U

Table 1 Properties of Ionic Compounds

Property	Cause	Explanation
hardness		
high melting temperature		
crystal structure		
form electrolytes		
conductivity		

LEARNING TIP

Improving Definitions
You now have a definition for ionic compounds that is slightly different from the one you were given in earlier grades. As you learn more about a concept, you will continue to enhance and improve your definition.

Molecular Elements and Compounds

Textbook pp. 61–69

Vocabulary

molecular element   covalent bond   bonding capacity   lone pair

diatomic   bonding electron   Lewis structure   structural formula

molecular compound

MAIN IDEA: Molecular elements and compounds differ from ionic elements and compounds in a variety of characteristic ways that include physical properties such as hardness and chemical properties, and how they bond.

1. Is the following statement true or false? If you think the statement is false, rewrite it to make it true: Like ionic compounds, molecular compounds have as their smallest subunit a structure of thousands of molecules. K/U

2. Which statement is true of molecular compounds? K/U
   (a) All molecules of a molecular compound are identical in structure, but different molecular compounds have molecules with different structures.
   (b) All molecules of a molecular compound are identical in formula, but different molecules in a molecular compound can have a different structure.
   (c) All molecules of a molecular compound are identical in structure, but each molecule in a molecular compound has a different formula.
   (d) All molecules of a molecular compound have the same number of each kind of atom, but each molecule in a molecular compound has a different structure.

3. Molecular compounds are usually made up of atoms that are _____, while ionic compounds include both metals and non-metals. K/U

4. Unlike ionic compounds, most molecular compounds usually have _____ melting points and have _____ solubility in water. K/U

5. (a) How is bonding capacity related to the number of valence electrons that an element has?

   (b) Create a formula for finding the bonding capacity of an element, given the number of electrons in its valence shell. Explain how your formula works and give an example. K/U C A

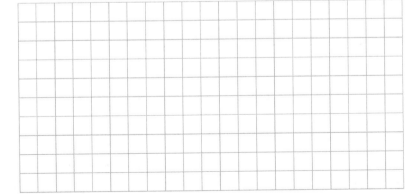

LEARNING TIP

Co-valent
Note that the prefix *co-* typically means "with" or "shared" in words such as cooperate and cohabitate. The term "covalent" implies "sharing its valence" or "sharing electrons."

6. Define "lone pair." K/U

MAIN IDEA: Lewis structures and structural formulas show how compounds form.

7. How is a Lewis structure different from a Lewis diagram? K/U

   (a) A Lewis structure uses only dashes for electrons, while a Lewis diagram uses only dots.

   (b) A Lewis structure uses only dashes for bonds and dots for electrons, while a Lewis diagram uses dots only.

   (c) A Lewis structure uses only dashes for bonds, while a Lewis diagram uses dots for bonds.

   (d) A Lewis structure uses dashes only, while a Lewis diagram uses both dashes and dots.

8. How are covalent bonds different from ionic bonds? K/U

LEARNING **TIP**

Lewis Symbols and Lewis Structures
Both Lewis symbols and Lewis structures show the chemical symbols of elements and the valence electrons of each atom. So what is the difference? In Section 1.5 you learned that a Lewis symbol represents an atom or ion of an element. A Lewis structure, however, shows how bonds form between two or more atoms to form a molecule. The lines represent covalent bonds.

9. Write a Lewis structure and a structural formula for carbon dioxide, CO_2. T/I

LEARNING **TIP**

Exceptions to the Rule
As we develop a better understanding of chemical concepts, our models and rules improve. The octet rule is very helpful as we start to draw and visualize molecules. There are exceptions, however, that we cannot explain at this stage. Indeed, there are oddities and exceptions even with the best present-day models. Scientific knowledge is always evolving and there is definitely room for future discoveries.

10. Write a Lewis structure and a structural formula for the phosphate ion, $[PO_4]^{3-}$. T/I

11. Complete the Venn diagram (**Figure 1**) comparing ionic and molecular compounds. K/U C

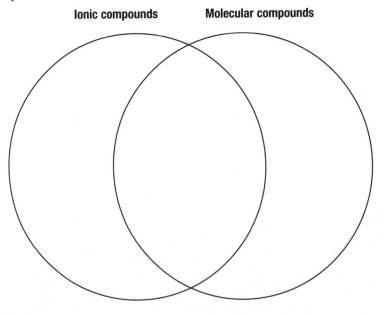

Ionic compounds   **Molecular compounds**

Figure 1

Chemical Bonding and Electronegativity

Textbook pp. 70–73

Vocabulary

electronegativity   electronegativity   non-polar covalent   polar covalent
                     difference (ΔEN)   bond   bond

MAIN IDEA: Electronegativity is a measure of how tightly an atom hangs on to its bonding electrons.

1. Is the following statement true or false? If you think the statement is false, rewrite it to make it true: As the atomic radius of an atom increases, electronegativity increases. K/U

2. Within a single row of the periodic table, the element farthest to the _____ side will have the greatest electronegativity. K/U

3. Which of the following statements best explains the low electronegativity value of sodium? K/U

   (a) Sodium can most readily reach a stable octet by getting rid of the single electron in its valence shell, so its hold on that electron is weak.

   (b) Sodium has only a few protons, so its electrons are only weakly attracted to its nucleus.

   (c) Sodium's hold on all of its electrons is weak because hard metals are more likely to form cations than soft metals.

   (d) Sodium has a small atomic radius, so it is more likely to give up electrons than an element with a large atomic radius like chlorine.

4. Complete **Table 1** to summarize electronegativity trends in the periodic table. K/U

> **STUDY TIP**
>
> **Characterizing Bonds**
> When categorizing bonds, keep the element's position on the periodic table in mind. Metals from the left side of the table are likely to have low ΔEN values, while non-metals from the right side of the table are likely to have high values.

Table 1 Electronegativity Trends

	Low electronegativity	High electronegativity
large atomic radius		
large ionic radius		
high first ionization energy		
location toward left side of periodic table		
location toward right side of periodic table		
location toward upper part of periodic table		
electron affinity		
metal		
forms diatomic molecules		

MAIN IDEA: Electronegativity difference helps determine whether a bond is covalent, polar-covalent, or ionic.

5. Which of the following best characterizes an ionic bond? K/U
   (a) two elements with the same electronegativity value
   (b) two elements with similar electronegativity values
   (c) two elements with very different electronegativity values
   (d) two elements with electronegativity values that have a difference of about 1.0

6. Is it possible for a diatomic molecule to have a polar-covalent bond? Why or why not? K/U

7. A compound consists of two different atoms that have an electronegativity difference of 1.4. K/U T/I
   (a) Would you classify this bond as non-polar, polar-covalent, or ionic? Explain.

   (b) Within its category, how would you classify this bond? Explain.

8. Complete **Table 2** to identify the characteristics of covalent, polar-covalent, and ionic compounds K/U

   Table 2 Covalent, Polar-Covalent, and Ionic Compounds

	Covalent compound	Polar-covalent compound	Ionic compound
ΔEN			
example			
atom with greater electronegativity			
"tug-of-war" winner			

9. Compare methanol and methane in **Figure 1**. Which molecule is likely to be more polar? How do you know? K/U T/I

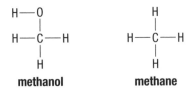

methanol   methane

Figure 1

Chemical Formulas and Nomenclature

Textbook pp. 74–81

Vocabulary

binary ionic compound   oxyanion   zero-sum rule   hydrate

polyatomic ionic compound

MAIN IDEA: The chemical formula for a compound can be determined by following a strict set of rules.

1. An ionic compound that is composed of exactly _____ different ions is called a binary ionic compound. K/U

2. Is the following statement true or false? If you think the statement is false, rewrite it to make it true: All compounds with an IUPAC name also have a common name. K/U

3. SO_4^{2-} is an example of which of the following? K/U
   (a) a binary polyatomic ion
   (b) a polyatomic ion that belongs to the oxyanion group
   (c) a polyatomic ion that belongs to the sulfite group
   (d) a binary ionic compound that belongs to the oxyanion group

4. In the ionic compound $X_2(YZ_4)_5$, the polyatomic ion YZ_4 has a charge of -2. What is the charge of the X ion? K/U T/I

5. Write a chemical formula for the following compounds. T/I C
   (a) calcium nitride

   (b) magnesium nitrate

   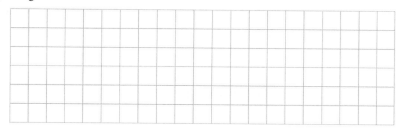

MAIN IDEA: The IUPAC chemical name for a compound can be determined by following a strict set of rules.

6. Write the IUPAC name of each compound. T/I
   (a) $CaFl_2$ _____
   (b) Al_2O_3 _____
   (c) Na_2S _____
   (d) ZnI_2 _____

LEARNING **TIP**

Ionic Charges
The ionic charges are usually written in the top right corner of each element's cell in the periodic table. You could also remember that all Group 1 elements form ions with a charge of $1+$, Group 2 ions have a charge of $2+$, Group 16 ions have a charge of $2-$, and Group 17 ions have a charge of $1-$.

LEARNING **TIP**

The Crisscross Method
You may have learned this alternative method for determining the charges on ions, given the formula of an ionic compound:

While the crisscross method can be a helpful tool, it is important to understand why it works, rather than simply memorizing how it works.

7. Write the IUPAC name for $Pb_3(PO_4)_2$. K/U T/I

8. Write the IUPAC name of each compound. T/I
   (a) $CuCl_2$ _____
   (b) $FeBr_2$ _____
   (c) $FeCl_3$ _____
   (d) $PbBr_4$ _____

9. Use the flow chart (**Figure 1**) to name the compounds given below. T/I

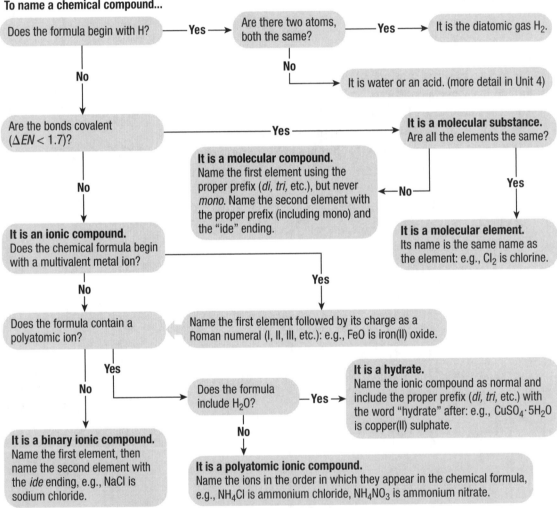

Figure 1

   (a) N_2O_5

   (b) CuF_2

   (c) $Al(NO_3)_3$

Sugar versus Artificial Sweeteners

Textbook pp. 82–83

MAIN IDEA: A variety of different sweeteners exist. Each sweetener has its dietary risks. The best policy is to limit intake of sweeteners.

1. Sugars have no nutritional value other than as a source of _____ for the body. K/U

2. Is the following statement true or false? If you think the statement is false, rewrite it to make it true: A glucose molecule is made of one molecule of sucrose joined with one molecule of fructose. K/U

3. How can you distinguish a carbohydrate sweetener from a non-carbohydrate sweetener? K/U

   (a) Carbohydrates are composed of carbon, oxygen, and hydrogen only, while non-carbohydrates include other types of atoms.
   (b) Carbohydrates are composed of carbon, oxygen, and hydrogen only, while non-carbohydrates are composed of carbon and hydrogen only.
   (c) Carbohydrate sweeteners are much sweeter than non-carbohydrate sweeteners.
   (d) Non-carbohydrate sweetener molecules are always much larger than carbohydrate sweetener molecules.

4. Compare sugar and sucralose. K/U T/I

   (a) Which substance is sweeter? How much more sweet?

   (b) Suppose you add 100 g of sucrose to a 1 L pitcher of ice tea for sweetening. To get the same level of sweetness, how much sucralose would you need to add to the same size container?

   (c) Some artificial sweeteners have more calories per gram than sugar. Why do you think artificial sweeteners are called "low-calorie" sweeteners?

5. Complete **Table 1** below to compare various sweeteners.

Table 1 Sweeteners

Sweetener	Sweetness (1–10)	Health benefits	Health risk
sucrose			
fructose			
sucralose			
aspartame			

Chemical Compounds and Bonding

The graphic organizer below summarizes some of the main ideas from Chapter 2. Fill in the blanks to complete the summary.

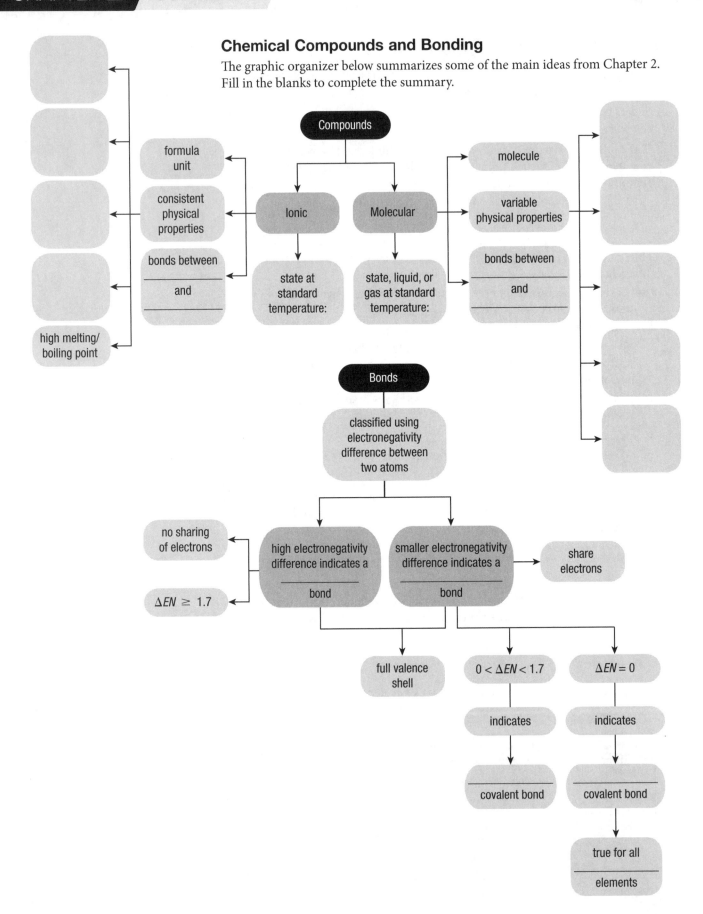

1. Is the following statement true or false? If you think the statement is false, rewrite it to make it true: The smallest unit of an ionic compound is the molecule. (2.1) K/U

K/U Knowledge/Understanding
T/I Thinking/Investigation
C Communication
A Application

2. Which of the following would you expect to have the greatest electronegativity difference? (2.3) K/U T/I
   (a) a group 1 metal and a group 15 gas
   (b) a group 2 metal and a group 17 liquid
   (c) a group 1 metal and a group 17 gas
   (d) a group 2 metal and a group 17 liquid

3. Complete **Table 1** to summarize the properties of ionic compounds. (2.1) K/U

Table 1 Properties of Ionic Compounds

Property	Typical ionic compound	Reason
texture		
melting point		
solubility in water		
electrical conduction		

4. Use the stem-and-leaf diagram (**Figure 1**) to rank ionic and molecular compounds by property. (2.2) K/U A

Property	Ionic Compounds
Hardness	
Flexibility	
Melting Point	
Boiling Point	
Ionizes in Solution	
Conducts in Solution	

Property	Molecular Compounds
Hardness	
Flexibility	
Melting Point	
Boiling Point	
Ionizes in Solution	
Conducts in Solution	

Figure 1

5. Draw Lewis symbols to show the formation of lithium oxide from lithium and oxygen. (2.1) C

6. Draw a Lewis structure and a structural formula for the compound SCl_2. (2.2) [c]

Lewis structure: Structural formula:

7. In the ionic compound X_4Y_3, the X cation has a charge of $3+$. What is the charge of the Y anion? (2.4) [K/U] [T/I]

8. Write the IUPAC name for the following compounds. (2.4) [K/U] [T/I]
   (a) K_2S _____
   (b) $Hg_3(PO_4)_2$ _____

9. Write the chemical formula for the following compounds. (2.4) [K/U] [T/I]
   (a) zinc chromate _____
   (b) lead(II) bromide _____

10. Compare ethane and acetic acid in **Figure 2**. Which molecule is more likely to dissolve in water? Explain. (2.3) [K/U] [T/I]

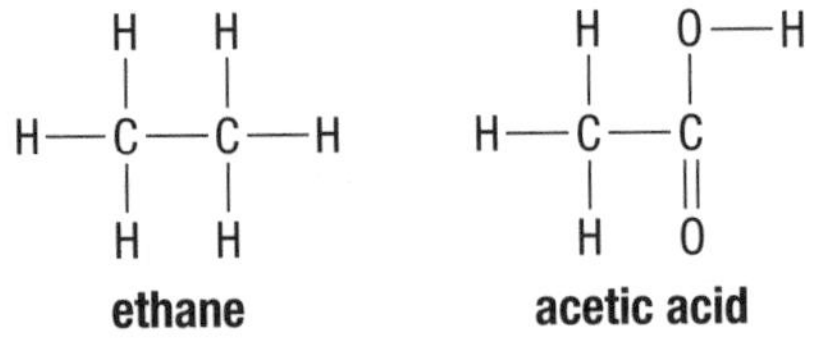

ethane   acetic acid

Figure 2

11. To reduce the amount of artificial sweetener she uses, a food chemist creates a solution that is half sucrose and half aspartame. She adds 19 g of this solution—half of the normal amount—to a bottle of pop. How successful is her compound likely to be? Explain. (2.5) [A]

Molecular Compounds

Textbook pp. 96–99

Vocabulary

renewable resource   petrochemical   biodegradable   upcycling

non-renewable resource   recycling   compostable

MAIN IDEA: The impact of molecular compounds on the environment largely depends on how they are created, what they are used for, and whether the compounds originate from renewable or non-renewable resources.

1. Major sources for molecular compounds include _____ and _____. K/U

2. Is the following statement true or false? If you think the statement is false, rewrite it to make it true: Fossil fuels are non-renewable resources because we have only a finite amount of them and they cannot be replaced once they are used. K/U

3. Fill in **Table 1** by classifying each of the resources as renewable or non-renewable; then explain each of your answers. K/U T/I

   Table 1 Renewable and Non-Renewable Resources

Resource	Renewable or non-renewable?	Explanation
newspaper		
coal		
plastic wrap		
blueberries		

> **STUDY TIP**
>
> **Molecular Compounds**
> Keep in mind that most molecular compounds are made of carbon and a few other elements, such as hydrogen and oxygen. For example, all plastics are made from petrochemicals that are almost entirely made of carbon and hydrogen.

MAIN IDEA: The impact that a compound has on the environment depends on whether it is reusable, recyclable, compostable, biodegradable, or upcyclable.

4. Which of the following best describes the difference between conventional plastic and biodegradable plastic? K/U

   (a) Conventional plastic is an artificial product. Biodegradable plastic is a natural product.

   (b) Conventional plastic cannot be recycled. Biodegradable plastic is recyclable.

   (c) Conventional plastic cannot be broken down by micro-organisms. Biodegradable plastic can be broken down by micro-organisms.

   (d) Conventional plastic can easily be broken down by micro-organisms. Biodegradable plastic cannot easily be broken down by micro-organisms.

5. Classify each of the materials in **Table 2**. K/U T/I

Table 2 Properties of Materials

Material	Reusable	Recyclable	Biodegradable	Compostable	Upcyclable
cotton					
steel					
leftover pizza					
plastic cellphone case					
pop bottle					
aluminum foil					
leather shoe					

6. List advantages and disadvantages for each process in the compare-and-contrast chart in **Figure 1**. K/U T/I

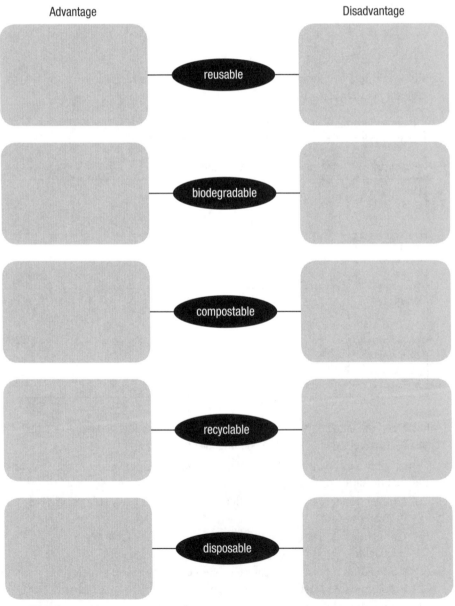

Figure 1

DEET in Insect Repellents

Textbook pp. 100–101

MAIN IDEA: All insect repellents are molecular compounds that have their own unique advantages, disadvantages, and risks.

1. The purpose of an insect _____ is to ward off insects while the purpose of a(n) _____ is to kill insects. K/U

2. What kinds of fabrics are likely to be damaged by DEET? K/U

3. Which of the following is the most critical problem in the use of DEET? K/U
   (a) whether DEET is effective in repelling insects
   (b) whether DEET is toxic to the environment
   (c) whether DEET harms wildlife as well as insects
   (d) whether DEET may cause seizures in adults who use it

4. To help organize your research, rank each issue in **Table 1** according to the importance it has for you. Give a reason for each of your choices. C A

Table 1 Issues and Ranking for Insect Repellents Featured in a Store

Issue	Rank	Reason
the concentration of insect repellent		
the active ingredient in the insect repellent		
the price of insect repellent		
how effective the product is		
reported health concerns about the product		
how well known the company is		
how safe the product is for children		

5. Which insect repellent are you likely to choose? Explain your choice. C A

Polar Bonds and Polar Molecules

Textbook pp. 102–108

> **Vocabulary**
>
> polar molecule   non-polar molecule

MAIN IDEA: Bond polarity depends on the electronegativity difference between bonding atoms. Molecular polarity depends on the molecule's shape, the character of its bonds, and the interaction between various parts of the molecule.

1. In a diatomic molecule with a polar covalent bond, the electrons tend to cluster more closely to the atom that is more _____. **K/U**

2. Is the following statement true or false? If you think the statement is false, rewrite it to make it true: Water gets its polar character primarily from the asymmetry of its bent-V shape. **K/U**

> **LEARNING TIP**
>
> **Reviewing Previous Material**
> When you see a reference to earlier material, it is a good idea to go back and reread it. In particular, make sure that you understand important definitions. Relevant vocabulary here includes *polar covalent bond; non-polar covalent bond;* and *electronegativity difference, ΔEN.*

3. What would likely occur if a thin stream of a non-polar liquid were to pass near a vinyl strip that is negatively charged? **K/U**
   (a) The liquid would bend toward the charged strip.
   (b) The liquid would follow a straight path and not bend toward the charged strip.
   (c) The liquid would bend in a direction away from the charged strip.
   (d) The liquid would follow a straight path but the charged strip would bend toward the liquid.

4. In **Figure 1**, three pairs of atoms that form covalent bonds are shown with the electronegativity value of each atom provided. **K/U** **T/I**

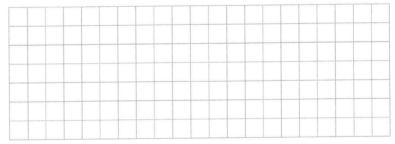

C = 2.6   Cl = 3.2   C = 2.6   C = 2.6   C = 2.6   H = 2.2

Figure 1

   (a) Calculate the electronegativity difference between each pair of atoms.

   (b) Use electronegativity to rank the bonds from most polar to least polar.

   (c) Draw in the electron "cloud" for each atom, indicating electron density. Label your diagrams with "δ" symbols to show positive and negative poles.

MAIN IDEA: Electronegativity differences, molecule shape, and Lewis structures can be used to determine the polarity of a molecular compound.

5. Determine whether HCl is polar or non-polar. T/I

6. Determine whether H_2 is polar or non-polar. T/I

7. Determine whether NF_3 is polar or non-polar. T/I

8. Determine whether CO_2 is polar or non-polar. [T/I]

9. The NO_2 molecule has a bent shape (**Figure 2**). Determine whether NO_2 is polar or non-polar. [T/I]

Figure 2

Intermolecular Forces

Vocabulary

intermolecular force   London dispersion   van der Waals   hydrogen
dipole-dipole force   force   forces   bond

Textbook pp. 109–115

MAIN IDEA: A variety of intermolecular forces hold substances together. These forces include ionic bonds in ionic compounds, and dipole-dipole forces, London dispersion forces, and hydrogen bonds in molecular compounds.

1. Ionic compounds are held together by the _____ of the elements that make up the compound, not by _____ forces. [K/U]

2. Is the following statement true or false? If you think the statement is false, rewrite it to make it true: A dipole-dipole force is a special form of hydrogen bond. [K/U]

3. What conclusion can you draw from the fact that all substances, even noble gases, will assume a liquid state if they are cooled enough? [K/U]
   (a) A strong repulsive force exists between particles of all substances at high temperatures.
   (b) Covalent bonds will attract one another at very low temperatures.
   (c) Cooling a substance increases dipole-dipole forces.
   (d) Some attractive force exists between entities of all substances.

4. The melting point of a molecular compound depends primarily on how tightly its molecules are held together by the three _____ forces. [K/U]

5. Use **Table 1** to rank forces that hold compounds together according to strength. [T/I]

> **LEARNING TIP**
>
> **International Interactions**
> The prefix *inter-* is used in many contexts. Some familiar uses include "international," "intermission," and "interstellar." In each case, "inter" means "between." International treaties are agreements that exist between individual nations. Similarly, intermolecular forces are forces that exist between individual molecules.

Table 1 Properties of Elements

Rank	Type of force or bond	Causes	Example
1			
2			
3			
4			

MAIN IDEA: Ball and stick models of groups of molecules can reveal how intermolecular forces can determine physical properties, such as whether the compound is solid, liquid, or gas in standard conditions.

6. (a) Draw ball and stick models for HCl and H_2O.

(b) Which intermolecular force will arise between H and Cl in a group of HCl molecules?

(c) Draw a model of a group of HCl molecules and the intermolecular forces between them.

(d) Draw a model of a group of water molecules and the intermolecular forces between them. T/I

7. The iodine molecule, I_2, has a melting point of 113.7 °C and a boiling point of 184.3 °C. C A
    (a) What is the electronegativity difference, ΔEN, between the two atoms in the I_2 molecule?

    (b) Is I_2 a polar molecule or a non-polar molecule?

    (c) How is it that the melting and boiling points of I_2 are higher than those of water, a highly polar molecule?

Hydrogen Bonding and Water

Vocabulary	
surface tension	

Textbook pp. 116–118

MAIN IDEA: Water has several properties that make it special and different from other molecular compounds. These properties include high melting and boiling points, high surface tension, low density when solid, and the ability to dissolve many substances.

1. Is the following statement true or false? If you think the statement is false, rewrite it to make it true: Water is the only compound that exists on Earth's surface in all three states: solid, liquid, and gas. K/U

LEARNING TIP

Hydrogen Bonds
Keep in mind that while hydrogen bonds can form as H-F, H-O, and H-N bonds, the most important hydrogen bonds include water because water is so much more abundant than any nitrogen or fluorine-containing compound on Earth.

---

2. Hot wax is heated to a liquid state. As the wax cools, where would you expect to find the first evidence of solid material? K/U
   (a) on the top of the liquid because wax is less dense than water
   (b) at the bottom of the liquid because solid wax is more dense than liquid wax
   (c) at the bottom of the liquid because liquid wax is more dense than solid wax
   (d) toward the top of the liquid because solid and liquid wax by definition must have the same density

3. A distant planet is discovered that has an average daily temperature range of between $-100\ ^\circ$C and $-50\ ^\circ$C. T/I
   (a) In what physical state would you expect to find the following compounds?
      (i) ammonia: _____
      (ii) hydrogen sulfide: _____
      (iii) water: _____
   (b) Of water, ammonia, and hydrogen sulfide, which compound would be more likely to support life on this planet? Explain.

4. A town beside a lake has an air temperature of $10\ ^\circ$C. The lake also has a temperature of $10\ ^\circ$C. A warm front comes in and raises the air temperature to $20\ ^\circ$C for a day. T/I
   (a) How would you expect the water temperature in the lake to change? Explain.
   (b) In general, how would you describe the consequences of water's specific heat capacity?

5. Fill in **Figure 1** to explain why water is special.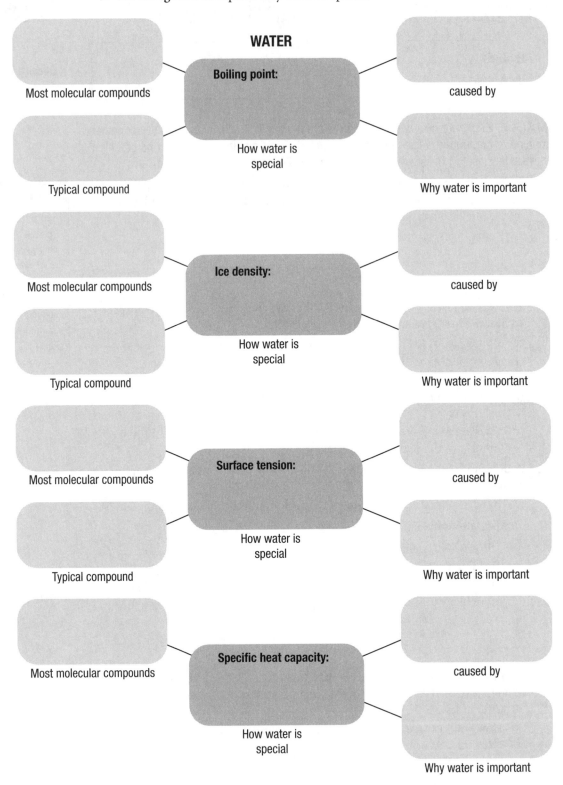

WATER

Most molecular compounds

Boiling point:

caused by

Typical compound

How water is
special

Why water is important

Most molecular compounds

Ice density:

caused by

Typical compound

How water is
special

Why water is important

Most molecular compounds

Surface tension:

caused by

Typical compound

How water is
special

Why water is important

Most molecular compounds

Specific heat capacity:

caused by

How water is
special

Why water is important

Figure 1

Green Chemistry in Action: Choosing the Right Materials

MAIN IDEA: In order to be considered "green," a product must be sustainable, safe for the environment, non-polluting, and not require fossil fuels for production. The product must also end its life in a manner that is not harmful to the environment.

Textbook pp. 119–122

1. Is the following statement true or false? If you think the statement is false, rewrite it to make it true: Green chemistry aims to identify negative effects that compounds may have on the environment before they are released in the environment. K/U

2. Complete the Venn diagram in **Figure 1** to compare bioplastics with conventional plastics. K/U

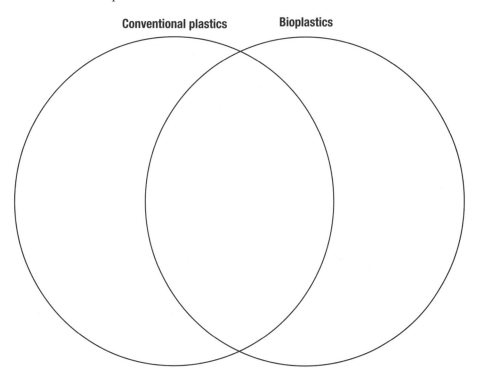

Conventional plastics   **Bioplastics**

Figure 1

3. Match the property on the left with the most appropriate description on the right. The properties may be used more than once. K/U

   (a) biodegradation
   (b) composting

   (i)   concerned with creating a useful end product
   (ii) involves the breakdown of the material
   (iii) is important to landfills

4. Which of the following statements casts doubt on how environmentally friendly PLA bioplastics actually are? K/U
   (a) PLA production does not use any less fossil fuels than the production of conventional plastics.
   (b) PLA plastics are not compostable unless their temperature is raised to 55 °C, something that requires energy consumption.
   (c) PLA plastics are not compostable at any temperature.
   (d) PLA plastics are not compostable unless their temperature is raised to 55 °C and they are mixed with a variety of toxic compounds.

5. Complete **Table 1** to compare conventional products to green products. K/U

Table 1 Conventional vs. Green Products

Step	Conventional product requirement	Green product requirement	Advantage of green product
raw materials			
production process			
product function			
by-products			
end-of-product life			

6. The following statements describe how plastic computer cases are being designed to be more environmentally friendly. Number the statements from 1 to 6 to show the correct sequence. K/U
   ____ Increased kinetic energy can overwhelm intermolecular forces between molecules in a plastic.
   ____ This can melt, deform, or decompose plastic computer cases.
   ____ Since they do not break down easily, BFRs cause environmental problems.
   ____ Computers can generate a great deal of thermal energy.
   ____ As an alternative to BFRs, scientists are developing bioplastics that can withstand high temperatures yet can be biodegraded.
   ____ To prevent damage, chemists use BFR plastics for computer cases that can withstand high temperatures.
   ____ Thermal energy increases kinetic energy in solid materials.

7. How would you feel about imposing a "disposal cost" for disposable diapers when they are purchased? State your opinion. C A

Molecular Compounds and Intermolecular Forces

The graphic organizer below summarizes some of the main ideas from Chapter 3.
Fill in the blanks and add notes to create your own study tool.

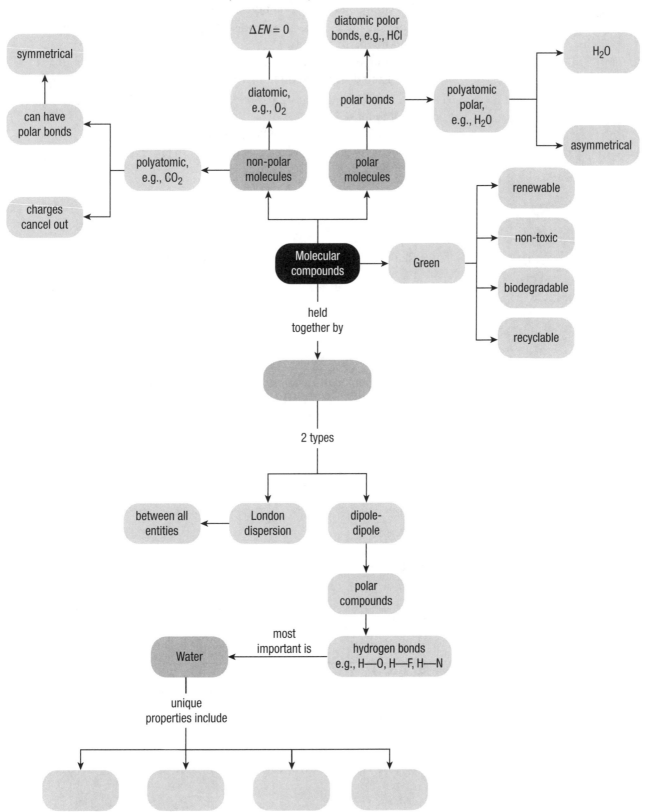

1. Which properties of a compound that is used as an insect repellent does a chemist look for? (3.2) **K/U**
   (a) The compound is effective at killing insects but does not harm humans.
   (b) The compound mimics natural compounds that kill insects.
   (c) The compound is effective in preventing insects from reproducing but does not harm humans.
   (d) The compound masks the scent of a human or has a scent that insects avoid and does not harm humans.

2. Are the following statements true or false? If you think the statement is false, rewrite it to make it true. **K/U**
   (a) The crystalline structure of liquid water takes up more space than the structure of solid water, causing water to take up more space when it freezes. (3.5)

   (b) Raindrops form as beads because of the high value of water's surface tension that is caused by the strong oxygen bonds that form between water molecules. (3.5)

3. A chemist is looking to create a new plastic compound that can be used to strengthen paper towels so they last a long time. Rank each property in **Table 1** for this compound. Then explain your thinking. (3.1) **C**

   Table 1 Properties for Paper Towel Plastic

Property	Rank of importance	Explanation
reusable		
biodegradable		
compostable		
recyclable		
upcyclable		

4. (a) Complete **Figure 1** to show the behaviour of a thin stream of each of the compounds shown being released near a negatively charged acetate strip.

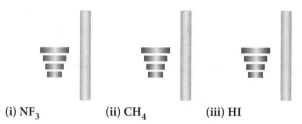

(i) NF$_3$ (ii) CH$_4$ (iii) HI

Figure 1

(b) Explain your answers to part (a) above. (3.3) K/U

5. Melting and boiling point data for compounds KCl, SCl$_2$, HF, and N$_2$ are shown in **Table 2**. Identify each compound. Then identify the force that is primarily responsible for holding the entities together in each compound. (3.4) K/U

Table 2 Unknown Compounds

Compound	Melting point (°C)	Boiling point (°C)	Force
	−121 °C	59 °C	
	−210 °C	−196 °C	
	770 °C	1420 °C	
	−83 °C	20 °C	

6. Rank conventional plastics and bioplastics from 1–5 for each property, where 5 is best and 1 is poor. (3.6) K/U

(a) biodgradable   ____ conventional plastic   ____ bioplastic
(b) function   ____ conventional plastic   ____ bioplastic
(c) fossil fuel use   ____ conventional plastic   ____ bioplastic
(d) cost   ____ conventional plastic   ____ bioplastic
(e) greenhouse emissions ____ conventional plastic   ____ bioplastic
(f) compostable   ____ conventional plastic   ____ bioplastic

K/U Knowledge/Understanding
T/I Thinking/Investigation
C   Communication
A   Application

1. Which of the following best describes Bohr's contribution to atomic theory? (1.1) K/U
   (a) Excited atoms that emit electrons give off energy only at certain levels, indicating that electrons can exist only at discrete energy levels.
   (b) Excited atoms that emit protons give off energy only at certain levels, indicating that atoms can exist only at specific energy levels.
   (c) Excited atoms that emit electrons give off energy at a variety of different levels, indicating that electrons orbit the nucleus in circular paths.
   (d) Excited atoms that emit electrons give off energy at a variety of different levels, indicating that electrons can exist at any energy level.

2. (a) Draw a Bohr–Rutherford diagram of oxygen.

   (b) Draw a second diagram to show how an oxygen atom ionizes. Label the diagram and show its charge. (1.3) T/I

3. Is the following statement true or false? If you think the statement is false, rewrite it to make it true: The electronegativity difference between carbon and fluorine is 1.4, indicating that a C-F bond is ionic in character. (2.3) K/U

4. $A_2(BC_3)_4$ is an ionic compound. (2.4) K/U T/I
   (a) Identify the anion for this compound. What kind of anion is this?

   (b) The cation for this compound is multivalent. If the charge on the anion is −2, what is the valence of the cation?

5. Write the IUPAC name for the following compounds. (2.4) K/U T/I
   (a) $ZnBr_2$

   (b) Pb_3P_4

6. Write the chemical formula for the following compounds. (2.4) K/U T/I

   (a) lithium oxide

   (b) copper(II) nitride

7. Melting and boiling point data for compounds HCl, CaCl$_2$, NH$_3$, and O$_2$ are shown in the four diagrams of **Figure 2**. Identify each compound. Then identify the force that is primarily responsible for holding the entities together in each compound (3.4) K/U

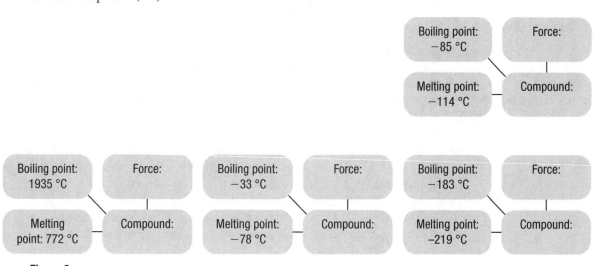

Figure 2

8. Which properties of water are unique? Write "special" or "not special" next to each item. (3.5) K/U

   (a) Water exists as a liquid at room temperature.
   (b) Water exists as a solid, liquid, and gas on Earth's surface.
   (c) Water expands when it freezes.
   (d) Water is a common compound with a melting point of over –10 °C.
   (e) Water is a molecular compound with a boiling point of over 80 °C.
   (f) Water as a solid floats on liquid water.
   (g) Water forms droplets.

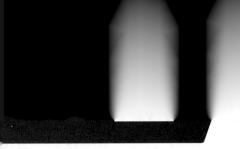

BIG IDEAS

- Chemicals react in predictable ways.
- Chemical reactions and their applications have significant implications for society and the environment.

Chapter 4: The Effects of Chemical Reactions

Chemical reactions occur all around us. Evidence that a chemical reaction has occurred includes the following: colour change, absorption or release of energy, production of a gas, and/or formation of a precipitate. Chemical equations must be balanced to obey the law of conservation of mass.

Chemical reactions can be grouped based on the patterns that occur in the reaction. Synthesis reactions combine two smaller elements to make a larger more complex compound and are represented by $A + B \rightarrow AB$. Decomposition reactions include the breakdown of a complex reactant into smaller parts and are represented by the general equation $AB \rightarrow A + B$.

Single displacement reactions are another type of chemical reaction in which one single element displaces another in a compound: $A + BC \rightarrow AC + B$. Replacement in these types of reactions is based on the activity series in which elements range from most reactive at the top, to least reactive at the bottom. Double displacement reactions involve the rearrangement of two reactants to form two new products: $AB + CD \rightarrow AD + CB$. Double displacement reactions form a precipitate, a neutralized solution, or a gas. Precipitates that form can be predicted using a solubility table.

Chapter 5: Chemical Processes

Hydrocarbons are compounds comprised of carbon and hydrogen. Combustion of hydrocarbons can be complete or incomplete. Complete combustion produces the most energy efficiency and the fewest waste products. Incomplete combustion results in the production of soot, carbon monoxide, and water.

Non-metallic oxides form acidic solutions in water. Metallic oxides form basic solutions in water. Acidity from carbon, nitrogen, and sulfur oxides causes considerable environmental harm. Acids can be neutralized by hydroxide or carbonate compounds. Highly acidic compounds produce excess hydrogen ions, while highly basic compounds produce excess hydroxide ions. Neutralization agents are selected based on their safety, appropriateness, and cost.

Mining is a process whereby minerals are removed from the ground. Metallurgy is a process of refining the minerals to obtain the metals. Flotation is one method used to concentrate ore, and smelting is used to extract metal from ore. Flash smelting is more efficient than traditional smelting, offering a host of environmental benefits. Acid mine drainage is a significant environmental threat posed by mining operations.

Remediation is used to remove contaminants from land or water so that the land can be used again. Remediation technologies can include physical strategies (flushing), chemical strategies (stabilization and solidification), and biological strategies. Bioremediation is a unique type of remediation that can create less environmental harm than physical or chemical remediation strategies. Phytoremediation is a specific type of bioremediation strategy that uses plants to help remove toxins from the soil or water.

Introduction to Chemical Reactions

Vocabulary

chemical reaction   precipitate   catalyst   law of conservation of mass

Textbook pp. 152–155

MAIN IDEA: Chemical reactions transform one substance into new or different substance(s).

1. When does a physical change in a substance occur? K/U

2. When does a chemical change in a substance occur? K/U

3. Classify the reactions listed in **Table 1** as producing either a chemical change or a physical change. T/I A

   Table 1 Chemical and Physical Changes

The reaction	Type of change that occurred
Water is heated in a pot on the stove and becomes vaporized.	
Water and metal react to form rust.	
A snowball melts in your hand.	
Hydrogen peroxide is mixed with water to form hydrogen and oxygen gas.	

   STUDY TIP

   Examine Your Environment
   Physical and chemical changes occur all around us. Observe substances in your everyday life and classify their reactions as physical or chemical.

4. Acid is placed on metal, producing a change in the colour of the metal, a release of a gas, a release of thermal energy, and a solid residue. Which of these clues indicates that a chemical reaction has taken place? K/U T/I

5. Water is boiled on a stove, producing a gas. A
   (a) Has a chemical change occurred? _____
   (b) How do you know? What would you do to prove it?

6. The solid produced in the reaction liquid + liquid → solid is called a _____ K/U

MAIN IDEA: During a chemical reaction, reactant atoms rearrange themselves to form products. A balanced chemical equation gives the correct proportions of chemicals in a chemical reaction.

7. Complete **Table 2** below with regard to the following chemical reaction, noting if the chemical is a reactant, product, or catalyst. [T/I]

$$CH_2CH_2OH + HCl \xrightarrow{H_2SO_4} CH_3CH_2Cl + H_2O$$

Table 2 Identification of Materials

Chemical	Description
CH_2CH_2OH	
HCl	
H_2SO_4	
CH_3CH_2Cl	
H_2O	

8. In the reaction below, the mass of the reactant equals the mass of the products.

$$H_2CO_3 \rightarrow H_2O + CO_2$$

This concept is known as _____. [K/U]

9. Chemical equations include notations following each compound. These notations indicate the state of the compound. Complete **Table 3** to show what each state symbol means. [K/U]

Table 3 Identification of State Symbol

State symbol	Meaning
s	
l	
g	
aq	

10. Complete **Table 4** by developing a word equation, skeleton equation, and balanced chemical equation for splitting water into its component parts: oxygen and hydrogen. [T/I]

Table 4 Balancing Equations

word equation	
skeleton equation	
balanced chemical equation	

11. Balance the following chemical equations. [T/I]

(a) $CH_4(g) + O_2(g) \rightarrow CO_2(g) + H_2O(l)$

(b) $Mg(s) + O_2(g) \rightarrow MgO(s)$

(c) $Fe(s) + Cl_2(g) \rightarrow 2\ FeCl_3(aq)$

(d) $C_2H_6(g) + O_2(g) \rightarrow CO_2(g) + H_2O(l)$

Synthesis and Decomposition Reactions

Textbook pp. 156–161

4.2

> **Vocabulary**
>
> synthesis reaction   decomposition reaction

MAIN IDEA: Patterns in types of chemical reactions can be used to predict the products of reactions. Synthesis reactions are represented by the general formula A + B → AB. Decomposition reactions are represented by the general formula AB → A + B. Comparison of synthesis and decomposition reactions shows that these two reactions are opposites of each other.

1. Elements that appear in the same columns of the periodic table will have similar _____. K/U

   (a) appearances

   (b) reactivity

   (c) names

   (d) chemical formulas

2. Potassium is an alkali metal that reacts readily with chlorine. Name two other elements that will react with chlorine. K/U

3. Describe what occurs in a synthesis reaction. K/U

4. Complete **Table 1** for a synthesis reaction involving sodium and oxygen to form sodium oxide. Remember to consider the ionic charge of each element in determining the final product. (Hint: Sodium is +1 and oxygen is −2.) T/I

   Table 1 Synthesis Reaction for Sodium and Oxygen

word equation	
skeleton equation	
balanced chemical equation	

5. Is the following statement true or false? If you think the statement is false, rewrite it to make it true: Group 1 elements, which include alkali metals, typically form molecular compounds. K/U

LEARNING TIP

Diatomic Elements
Several non-metallic elements occur naturally as diatomic molecules. These include hydrogen and the elements of the fluorine "corner" of the periodic table:

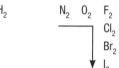

STUDY TIP

The Periodic Table
Take a minute to look at the periodic table. The vertical columns on the table represent groups of elements that have similar properties. These properties help to predict the outcomes of a chemical reaction. For example:

$$2 K + Cl_2 \rightarrow 2 KCl$$

Using elements in the same groups (columns), it is possible to predict that

$$2 Na + Br_2 \rightarrow 2 NaBr$$

STUDY TIP

Diatomic Molecules
Remember some molecules such as hydrogen, oxygen, chlorine, and bromine occur naturally as diatomic elements. This will impact equation balancing.

6. Molecular compounds are made up of _____. K/U

7. Complete and balance the following equations for synthesis reactions in Table 2. T/I

Table 2 Completing and Balancing Equations for Synthesis Reactions

Reactants	Product	Balanced equation
$N_2(g) + H_2(g)$		
$Li(s) + Cl_2(g)$		
$Al(s) + Br_2(g)$		
$K(s) + S(s)$		

8. Synthesis reactions can be difficult to predict. Why? T/I

LEARNING TIP

Opposite Reactions
Note that the patterns of decomposition reactions and synthesis reactions are opposites of each other.

9. Which of the following would be considered green sources of energy? K/U A
   (a) solar power
   (b) wind turbines
   (c) the combustion of gasoline
   (d) both a and b

10. Is the following statement true or false? If you think the statement is false, rewrite it to make it true: When water comes in contact with air, carbon dioxide in the air dissolves the water to form carbonic acid. K/U

11. Describe what occurs in a decomposition reaction. K/U

12. Describe opposite reactions in terms of synthesis and decomposition reactions. K/U

13. Complete **Table 3** for a decomposition reaction involving hydrogen chloride gas reduced to hydrogen and chloride. Remember: hydrogen and chloride are diatomic elements in their natural state. T/I

Table 3 A Decomposition Reaction

word equation	
skeleton equation	
balanced chemical equation	

14. Complete and balance the following equations for decomposition reactions in **Table 4**. T/I

Table 4 Completing and Balancing Equations for Decomposition Reactions

Reactant	Products	Balanced equation
$Ni_2O_3(s)$		
$Al_2O_3(s)$		
$Ca_3P_2(s)$		
$Na_2CO_3(s)$		

> **STUDY TIP**
>
> **Synthesis and Decomposition**
> Synthesis includes combining two or more products into one. Decomposition involves breaking one reactant into two products.

15. Identify each of the reactions in **Table 5** as either a synthesis reaction or a decomposition reaction. T/I

Table 5 Types of Reactions

Reaction	Type
$H_2CO_3(aq) \rightarrow H_2O(l) + CO_2(g)$	
$2\ Mg(s) + 2\ O_2(g) \rightarrow 2\ MgO(s)$	
$H_2SO_3(aq) \rightarrow H_2O(l) + SO_2(g)$	
$2\ P(s) + 3\ Cl_2(g) \rightarrow 2\ PCl_3(g)$	

Explore an Issue in Chemical Reactions

Textbook pp. 162–163

Garbage Gasification—A Heated Debate

MAIN IDEA: Environmental problems are a growing concern in modern society. Finding solutions for environmental issues such as waste management creates a number of benefits and drawbacks. Decision making requires an examination of all issues to outline the best solution.

1. What is gasification? K/U

STUDY TIP

Consider Your Community
Communities face ongoing challenges in meeting the needs of citizens. What environmental issues have been debated in your community? How do they impact the environment and human life?

---

2. Syngas is a mixture of hydrogen and carbon monoxide. The transformation of large compounds into the component parts of syngas represents what type of chemical reaction? K/U _____

3. Syngas can be used to create methanol, $CH_3OH(g)$. T/I
   (a) What type of reaction is this? _____
   (b) Write a skeleton equation for this reaction.

   (c) Write a balanced equation for this reaction.

4. Determining the solution for an environmental problem requires a number of steps for critical thinking. What is included in this process? K/U

STUDY TIP

Environmental Decision Making
Making the right decision for the environment requires a review of all the issues involved. Benefits and drawbacks of new technologies must be weighed against costs and impacts on human and animal health.

---

5. Gasification has both benefits and drawbacks. K/U T/I
   (a) Complete **Table 1** below identifying the benefits and drawbacks of gasification.

   Table 1 Benefits and Drawbacks of Gasification

Benefits of gasification	Drawbacks of gasification

   (b) What are some of the hazardous materials that are created by the process of gasification?

Single Displacement Reactions

Vocabulary

single displacement reaction

activity series

Textbook pp. 164–169

MAIN IDEA: Single displacement reactions occur when one element replaces another element in a compound, resulting in a new element and a new compound. Element A displaces element B from compound BC. This results in the production of a new compound, AC, and a new element B. A general pattern for a single displacement reaction is: $A + BC \rightarrow AC + B$.

1. Name one specific instance in which single displacement reactions can be useful. K/U

2. (a) Complete **Table 1** for a single displacement reaction involving zinc and copper chloride. In this reaction, zinc displaces copper.

Table 1 A Single Displacement Reaction

word equation	
skeleton equation	
balanced chemical equation	

(b) In this reaction, solid copper is formed. This is known as a
_____. T/I

STUDY TIP

Ionic Charge
When completing single displacement reactions, do not forget the ionic charge of the elements in the skeleton equation.

MAIN IDEA: An activity series ranks metals in order of reactivity from highest to lowest. It is used to summarize reactions of metals and single displacement reactions.

3. Complete and balance the following equations for single displacement reactions. K/U C A

(a) Reactants: $Mg(s) + HCl(l)$

Products:

Balanced equation:

(b) Reactants: $Zn(s) + H_2SO_4(l)$

Products:

Balanced equation:

(c) Reactants: $Cu(s) + AgNO_3(aq)$

Products:

Balanced equation:

4. Describe an activity series in your own words. K/U C

STUDY TIP

Activity Series
When trying to determine if a displacement reaction will occur, look at the two metals involved in the reaction. If the more active metal is the element, the reaction will proceed. If the more active metal is part of the compound, no reaction will occur.

5. Is the following statement true or false? If you think the statement is false, rewrite it to make it true: The least reactive metals are at the top of the activity series. K/U

6. Activity series provide some generalizations about single displacement reactions. What are two important generalizations about activity series? K/U

7. **Figure 1** shows two activity series. K/U T/I

Metals	Decreasing Activity	Halogens
lithium potassium calcium sodium magnesium aluminum zinc chromium iron nickel tin lead HYDROGEN* copper mercury silver platinum gold		fluorine chlorine bromine iodine

Figure 1 Two activity series

(a) In a single displacement reaction, will potassium replace sodium? Why or why not?

(b) In a single displacement reaction, will platinum replace chromium? Why or why not?

(c) Determine if the reactions in **Table 2** will occur. If a reaction will occur, list the products. If no reaction occurs, state "no reaction."

Table 2 Single Displacement Reactions

Reaction	Products
$Al_2O_3(aq) + 2 Fe(s) \rightarrow$	
$2 Al(s) + Fe_2O_3(aq) \rightarrow$	
$Cl_2(g) + 2 KBr(aq) \rightarrow$	
$Al(s) + MgCl_2(aq) \rightarrow$	

8. Why is hydrogen included in the metal activity series? K/U
   (a) It forms a positive ion.
   (b) It forms a negative ion.
   (c) It cannot react with other elements.
   (d) all of the above

9. Why is predicting the reactivity of halogens (F, Cl, Br, and I) difficult? K/U

10. Predict the reaction that will occur in the following halogen reactions using **Figure 1** above. If a reaction occurs, list the products and balance the equation. If no reaction occurs, explain why not. T/I
    (a) $Cl_2(aq) + NaBr(aq) \rightarrow$

    (b) $Br_2(g) + KI(s) \rightarrow$

    (c) $Br_2(g) + 2 NaCl(aq) \rightarrow$

11. Acid indigestion is a common condition caused by excess stomach acid or HCl. In order to neutralize stomach acid, sodium hydrogen carbonate, $NaHCO_3$, is often used. Why is this compound effective for neutralizing stomach acid? T/I A

Chemistry JOURNAL

The Mystery of the Missing Mercury

MAIN IDEA: Single displacement reactions can be seen in the natural environment. An examination of the emergence and disappearance of mercury in the Arctic provides some insight into how displacement reactions work in practice.

1. Mercury disappears from the environment in the Arctic air during the spring. How does this process occur? K/U

2. Why does mercury remain in the environment for such a long time? (Hint: consider the activity series). K/U

3. Mercury does not naturally occur in the atmosphere, yet large amounts of it can be found in our environment. Why is there so much mercury in our environment? K/U

4. Research regarding the missing mercury in the Arctic is ongoing. Use the Internet to research some of the challenges that exist for furthering this research. T/I

5. Mercury that combines with carbon atoms poses a unique threat to human and animal health. Why? K/U A

Double Displacement Reactions

Vocabulary

double displacement reactions

solution

solute

solvent

solubility

neutralization reaction

Textbook pp. 172–177

MAIN IDEA: Double displacement reactions are reactions in which elements in two compounds (AB and CD) displace each other in order to form two new compounds (AD and CB). A general pattern for these reactions is AB + CD → AD + CB. In these reactions, a precipitate can be formed, a gas can be formed, or a neutralization reaction may occur.

1. A _____ is a homogeneous mixture of a solute dissolved in a solvent. K/U

   (a) precipitate

   (b) catalyst

   (c) solution

   (d) cation

2. Is the following statement true or false? If you think the statement is false, rewrite it to make it true: A substance is described as slightly soluble if a significant quantity of the substance dissolves. K/U

3. Complete **Table 1** for a double displacement reaction involving calcium carbonate and hydrochloric acid. K/U C A

   Table 1 Double Displacement Reaction for Calcium Carbonate and Hydrochloric Acid

word equation	
skeleton equation	
balanced chemical equation	

4. Complete and balance the following equations for double displacement reactions. T/I

   (a) Reactants: $KOH(l) + H_2SO_4(l)$

   Products:

   Balanced equation:

   (b) Reactants: $FeS(s) + HCl(l)$

   Products:

   Balanced equation:

   (c) Reactants: $NaCl(s) + H_2SO_4(l)$

   Products:

   Balanced equation:

> ## STUDY TIP
>
> **Double Displacement Reactions**
> Double displacement reactions occur when two ionic compounds split apart. In this process, an anion and cation are formed. Anions and cations can swap only if they produce products that will not break into anions and cations. In short, the products of the double displacement reaction will be more stable than the reactants.

5. Using the terms "solute" and "solvent," describe NaCl in the following equation:

$$NaCl(s) + H_2O(l) \rightarrow Na^-(aq) + Cl^+(aq) \quad \text{K/U}$$

MAIN IDEA: Double displacement reactions depend on the solubility of the products formed. In some instances, double displacement reactions will not occur.

6. Consider the reactions in **Table 2** and the solubility of the products. If a reaction will occur, list the products. If no reaction occurs, state "no reaction." T/I

Table 2 Double Displacement Reactions

Reaction	Products
$CaBr_2 + 2\ KOH \rightarrow$	
$Cu(OH)_2 + 2\ HC_2H_3O_2 \rightarrow$	
$FeS + 2\ HCl \rightarrow$	
$Ca(NO_3)_2 + 2\ HCl \rightarrow$	

STUDY TIP

Solubility
General rules for solubility can be used much in the same way that activity series are used for single displacement reactions. Solubility will indicate the likelihood of a double displacement reaction.

7. $AgCl(s)$ is reacted with KNO_3 in a test tube. No reaction occurs. Given that elements in both of these compounds can form anions and cations, explain why no reaction occured between these two compounds. T/I

8. Carbonic acid is often produced in double displacement reactions. Write the equation that shows how carbonic acid is decomposed into water and carbon dioxide. K/U C

MAIN IDEA: Neutralization reactions can be classified as double displacement reactions in which an acid reacts with a base. In these reactions an acid reacts with a base, producing a neutral solution. No precipitate is formed in these reactions.

9. How are neutralization reactions confirmed? K/U

10. Complete and balance the following equations for neutralization reactions. T/I
    (a) $HCl(l) + NaOH(aq) \rightarrow$

    (b) $H_2SO_4(l) + NH_4OH(l) \rightarrow$

    (c) $NaOH(aq) + H_2CO_3(l) \rightarrow$

Effects of Chemical Reactions

Chemical reactions are characterized by a number of properties. Common types of chemical reactions include synthesis, decomposition, single displacement reactions, and double displacement reactions. All chemical equations must be balanced due to the law of conservation of mass. The graphic organizer below summarizes some of the main ideas from Chapter 4. Fill in the blanks to create a study tool.

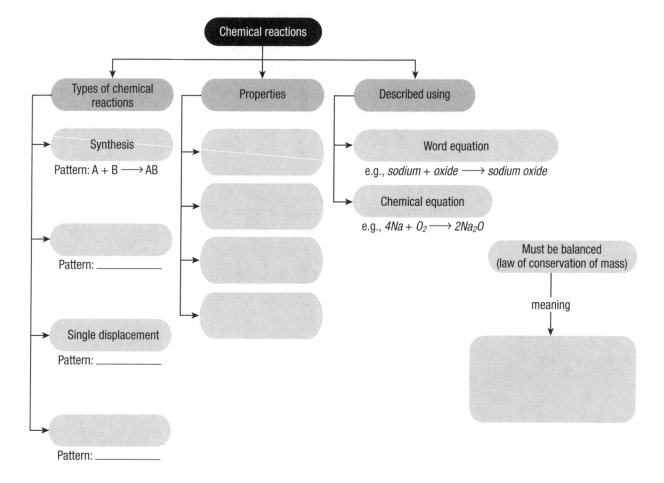

1. Which of the following is a balanced chemical equation? (4.1) **K/U**
   (a) $2 H_2CO_3(aq) \rightarrow H_2O(l) + 2 CO_2(g)$
   (b) $NaCl(s) + H_2SO_4(l) \rightarrow Na_2SO_4(s) + 2 HCl(l)$
   (c) $KOH(l) + H_2SO_4(l) \rightarrow K_2SO_4(s) + H_2O(l)$
   (d) $CaCO_3(s) + 2 HCl(l) \rightarrow CaCl_2(s) + H_2O(l) + CO_2(g)$

2. $4 Na(s) + O_2(g) \rightarrow 2 Na_2O(s)$ is what type of reaction? (4.1) **K/U**
   (a) synthesis
   (b) decomposition
   (c) single displacement
   (d) double displacement

3. Indicate whether each statement is true or false. If you think the statement is false, rewrite it to make it true.
   (a) Decomposition reactions begin with one reactant that is broken apart to form two products. (4.2) **K/U**

   (b) In a neutralization reaction, a precipitate is formed. (4.6) **K/U**

4. Explain the difference between single displacement reactions and double displacement reactions. (4.4, 4.6) **K/U**

5. In the following example of a single displacement reaction, no reaction occurs. Why? (4.4) **T/I**

$$Al(s) + MgCl_2(aq) \rightarrow$$

6. In the following example of a double displacement reaction, no reaction occurs. Why? (4.6) **T/I**

$$CaBr_2 + 2 KOH$$

7. A solid is added to an unknown solution. The addition produces a reaction in which energy is released, the solution changes colour, and a gas is released. (4.1) K/U

(a) Which of these indicates that a chemical reaction has occurred?

(b) What other observable change indicates that a chemical reaction has occurred?

(c) If no observable change occurred, what other test could be performed to determine the presence of a chemical reaction?

8. Complete **Table 1** with regard to the following chemical reaction, noting if the element or compound identified is a reactant, product, or catalyst: (4.1) C K/U

$$2 SO_2(g) + O_2(g) \xrightarrow{V_2O_5} 2 SO_3(g)$$

Table 1 Identification of Materials

Chemical	Description
2 SO$_3$	
2 SO$_2$	
V$_2$O$_5$	

9. Identify the type of reactions in **Table 2** based on the reactions identified in the graphic organizer above. (4.2, 4.4, 4.6) T/I

Table 2 Classification of Reactions

Reaction	Type
NaCO$_3$(s) $\rightarrow$ NaO(s) + CO$_2$(g)	
Zn(s) + CuCl$_2$(l) $\rightarrow$ ZnCl$_2$(l) + Cu(s)	
4 Na(s) + O$_2$(g) $\rightarrow$ 2 Na$_2$O(s)	
CaCO$_3$(s) + 2 HCl(l) $\rightarrow$ CaCl$_2$(s) + H$_2$O(l) + CO$_2$(g)	
2 KOH(l) + H$_2$SO$_4$(l) $\rightarrow$ K$_2$SO$_4$(s) + 2 H$_2$O(l)	

The Combustion of Hydrocarbons

Vocabulary

combustion   incomplete combustion   organic compound   complete combustion
                    of a hydrocarbon   of a hydrocarbon

greenhouse gas   air pollution

MAIN IDEA: Hydrocarbons are comprised of both hydrogen and carbon. These compounds are typically burned because they release energy during the combustion process.

1. Is the following statement true or false? If you think the statement is false, rewrite it to make it true: Combustion is a chemical reaction in which a fuel burns in oxygen, usually from air. **C**

> **STUDY TIP**
>
> **Combustion**
> Consider the last time you burned a candle. What did it look like? What colours did you see? Observations like these can provide an indication that a chemical reaction is occurring.

2. Combustion releases chemical energy in the form of _____ and _____. **K/U**

3. In addition to releasing chemical energy, the combustion of hydrocarbons also produces by-products including _____, _____, and _____. **K/U**

4. Carbon dioxide is unique because it is a greenhouse gas. Define "greenhouse gas" in your own words. **K/U** **C**

5. Organic compounds are so named because they contain what types of bonds? **K/U**
   (a) carbon-carbon bonds
   (b) carbon-hydrogen bonds
   (c) hydrogen-bonds
   (d) carbon-oxygen bonds

6. Which of the following three organic compounds include only hydrocarbons? **K/U** **A**
   (a) butane, propane, and methane
   (b) methane, lipids, and isopropyl alcohol
   (c) polysaccharides, lipids, and methanol
   (d) butane, formaldehyde, and acetone

7. What is air pollution? **K/U**

8. Is the following statement true or false? If you think the statement is false, rewrite it to make it true: Hydrocarbons are comprised of two specific elements, carbon and oxygen. **K/U**

MAIN IDEA: The combustion of hydrocarbons can be either complete or incomplete. Complete combustion of a hydrocarbon refers to the burning of a hydrocarbon in the presence of ample amounts of oxygen to produce carbon, dioxide, water, and energy. The incomplete combustion of a hydrocarbon refers to the burning of a hydrocarbon with a lack of oxygen present. When this occurs, by-products such as carbon monoxide, soot, water, and energy are created.

9. Complete combustion is the ideal method for burning a hydrocarbon. Why? K/U

10. Many hydrocarbons can be burned completely, including methane. Complete **Table 1** for the combustion of methane. K/U C

Table 1 The Complete Combustion of Methane

word equation	
skeleton equation	
balanced chemical equation	

11. A general formula for the complete combustion of a hydrocarbon is as follows:

$$C_xH_y + O_2(g) \rightarrow CO_2(g) + H_2O(l)$$

Complete **Table 2** below to determine the hydrocarbon reactant used in the complete combustion reaction. K/U T/I C

Table 2 Determine the Hydrocarbon

Reaction	Hydrocarbon
$2\ C_xH_y + 13O_2(g) \rightarrow 8\ CO_2(g) + 10\ H_2O(l)$	
$2\ C_xH_y + 7O_2(g) \rightarrow 4\ CO_2(g) + 6\ H_2O(l)$	
$C_xH_y + 5O_2(g) \rightarrow 3\ CO_2(g) + 4\ H_2O(l)$	
$C_xH_y + 11O_2(g) \rightarrow 8\ CO_2(g) + 6\ H_2O(l)$	

12. A welder decides to use an acetylene torch in a confined space to piece together a broken pipe. Although the torch is capable of reaching temperatures over 3500 °C, the welder is unable to repair the pipe with his torch. K/U T/I A

(a) What is the problem facing the welder in this case?

(b) What could the welder do to fix the pipe?

13. Flames produced from complete and incomplete combustion of hydrocarbons are different. K/U T/I

    (a) Describe the flames produced from the complete combustion of a hydrocarbon.

    (b) Describe the flames produced from the incomplete combustion of a hydrocarbon.

14. Incomplete combustion reactions often produce a wide range of by-products, including soot. Soot is represented in a chemical equation as _____. K/U

15. Incomplete combustion of hydrocarbons can result in multiple chemical equations, depending on the products produced. Assume that octane C_8H_{18}, is undergoing incomplete combustion. In one reaction, the products produced include soot and water. In the other reaction, the products produced include water and carbon monoxide. T/I

    (a) Write a skeleton equation for both reactions described above.

    (b) Write the balanced equations for the chemical reactions that you wrote in part (a).

    (c) Assume that octane undergoes a complete combustion reaction to produce only water and carbon dioxide. Write the skeleton and balanced equations for this chemical reaction.

16. Incomplete combustion poses a number of challenges. List three of the most pressing issues associated with incomplete combustion. K/U

The Role of Chance in Discovery

Textbook pp. 198–199

MAIN IDEA: Carefully designed experiments often produce unintended results. While these results are often dismissed as experimental error or bad luck, there are instances in which errors provide new products.

1. Many products have been discovered through the use of carefully designed experiments. Some products have been discovered through chance. Name three examples of products discovered by chance. K/U

2. Carefully designed experiments typically involve the use of a scientific process. What five steps are commonly used in the scientific research process? K/U C

3. Marie Curie discovered radiation by chance through her work with radioactive materials. Although Curie was credited with an important chance discovery, she ultimately paid the price for her discovery. Research what happened to Marie Curie as a result of her work with radioactive materials. K/U

4. Fill in **Table 1** to list some costs and benefits of chance discoveries. K/U T/I

Table 1 Costs and Benefits of Chance Discoveries

Costs	Benefits

5. What do you think a scientist should do when he or she discovers a new product by chance through the use of a planned experiment? T/I A

Elements and Their Oxides

Vocabulary

oxide	base	basic oxide
acid	acidic oxide	

MAIN IDEA: Metals and non-metals have different properties and form different oxides. Metals form basic oxides while non-metals form acidic oxides.

1. Non-metals and metals differ significantly in their physical properties. List at least three properties of each in **Table 1**. K/U

   Table 1 Properties of Metals and Non-Metals

Metals	Non-metals

2. Is the following statement true or false? If you think the statement is false, rewrite it to make it true: An oxide is a compound of any element combined with hydrogen. K/U

3. The oxidation of iron is a common reaction that produces rust, Fe_2O_3. Complete **Table 2** for this oxidation reaction. K/U T/I C

   Table 2 The Oxidation of Iron

word equation	
skeleton equation	
balanced chemical equation	

LEARNING TIP

Generic Oxides

If an element forms more than one compound with oxygen, we can refer to these compounds by the generic term "oxides." For example, nitrogen forms at least two different oxides: nitrogen monoxide and nitrogen dioxide.

4. Acids and bases have unique properties that distinguish them from one another. K/U T/I

   (a) Acids produce what types of ions in solution?

   (b) What properties do acids possess?

   (c) Write a general chemical equation for hydrochloric acid, HCl, added to water.

   (d) Bases produce what types of ions in solution?

   (e) What properties do bases possess?

   (f) Write a general chemical equation for sodium hydroxide added to water.

5. The pH scale is used to measure the acidity of a solution. K/U C

(a) A solution has a higher degree of acidity because of the _____
ions that are present.

(b) Complete **Table 3** below, indicating if the solutions are acids or bases.

Table 3 Acids and Bases

Solution	Acid or Base
vinegar	
detergent	
lemon juice	
bleach	
water	

6. Is the following statement true or false? If you think the statement is false, rewrite it to make it true: Non-metals react to form non-metallic oxides. When these non-metallic oxides are dissolved in water, they produce acidic solutions or acidic oxides. K/U

MAIN IDEA: Non-metals react to form acidic oxides and metals react to form basic oxides.

7. Predict if the products of the reactions in **Table 4** will be acidic or basic. K/U T/I C

Table 4 Acid or Base Product

Reaction	Acid or Base
$SO_2 + H_2O(l) \rightarrow$	
$Na_2O + H_2O(l) \rightarrow$	
$MgO + H_2O(l) \rightarrow$	
$Cl_2O_5 + H_2O(l) \rightarrow$	

8. Water generally has a pH of 7.0. However, rainwater has a pH of 5.6, indicating that it is slightly acidic. T/I A

(a) Why does rainwater from the atmosphere have a pH lower than 7.0?

(b) There are two chemical equations that demonstrate the formation of carbonic acid in an acidic solution Write them below.

(c) The conversion of carbonic acid producing a hydrogen atom is what type of reaction?
- (i) synthesis
- (ii) single displacement
- (iii) combustion
- (iv) decomposition

MAIN IDEA: Non-metallic oxides form acids that can be harmful to the environment and to human health. Metallic oxides form bases that can be used to reverse acidic conditions found in water and soil.

9. Nitrogen oxides are unique because of their reactivity in the environment. T/I C A

(a) Is the following statement true or false? If you think the statement is false, rewrite it to make it true: Nitrogen is a diatomic molecule that is stable because of the triple bonds that hold the nitrogen atoms together.

(b) Air drawn into a car's engine will contain stable amounts of diatomic nitrogen. However, under high temperatures in the engine, nitrogen undergoes a synthesis reaction with oxygen to form nitrogen oxide. Write a balanced equation for this reaction.

(c) Nitrogen oxide released from the car's exhaust will further react with oxygen to form nitrogen dioxide. Write a balanced equation for this reaction.

(d) Nitrogen dioxide further reacts with water in the atmosphere to form nitric acid (HNO_3) and nitrous acid (HNO_2). Write a balanced equation for this reaction.

(e) Cars are equipped with a catalytic converter to prevent the release of nitrogen dioxide by breaking it down into nitrogen and oxygen gas. Write a balanced equation for the decomposition reaction for nitrogen dioxide.

10. Acid rain occurs as a result of the production of carbonic acid in Earth's atmosphere. What are some of the effects of acid rain on plant, animal, and human life? T/I A

Neutralization Reactions

MAIN IDEA: Neutralization reactions are a specific type of double displacement reaction in which acids and bases are combined to form water and an ionic compound. The resulting solution should have a pH that is neutral or close to 7.

Textbook pp. 205–211

1. Complete the neutralization reactions in **Table 1** below. (Hint: Dissociate the acids and bases to form water and complete the decomposition reaction. Make sure to balance the equations.) K/U T/I

Table 1 Completing Neutralization Reactions

Reactants	Products
$HCl + NaOH \rightarrow$	
$H_2SO_4 + 2\ NH_4OH \rightarrow$	
$Ca(OH)_2 + H_2CO_3 \rightarrow$	
$HNO_3 + KOH \rightarrow$	
$H_3PO_4 + 3\ NaOH \rightarrow$	

MAIN IDEA: Neutralization reactions can be used in industrial processes to reduce the acidity of solutions. These reactions can be useful for protecting the environment from acidic and basic waste materials.

2. **Figure 1** provides an overview of a titration involving sodium hydroxide, NaOH, and phenolphthalein. HCl is added to the solution. A

(a) What are the colours for A and B in Figure 1?

(b) If acid is added to the solution until the initial colour of the solution fades, what is the solution's final pH?

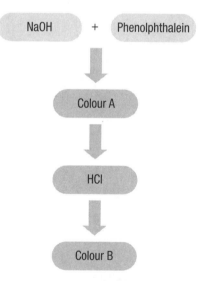

Figure 1 Titration of a base with an acid

MAIN IDEA: Neutralization reactions can be found all around us. Neutralization reactions occur when antacids are used to reduce excess stomach acid. Many household products also contain acids and bases.

3. Stomach acid (HCl) has a pH of about 1.5. For individuals who suffer from acid reflux, antacids or bases are commonly used to neutralize stomach acid. K/U T/I

(a) Write a balanced equation for the neutralization of stomach acid using calcium carbonate, $CaCO_3$.

(b) The products produced from this reaction include calcium chloride. Some antacids use sodium hydrogen carbonate. Write a balanced equation for the neutralization of stomach acid using sodium hydrogen carbonate, $NaHCO_3$.

(c) This produces sodium chloride, NaCl, as a by-product. Why is this compound problematic for human health?

4. Why is baking soda included as an ingredient in cookie recipes? T/I A

MAIN IDEA: Selecting the right neutralizing agent requires careful consideration. Factors that must be taken into consideration when selecting a neutralizing agent include safety, the reactant's cost, and its chemical properties.

5. Hydrochloric acid is a strong acid that may be effective for neutralizing a wide range of bases. However, it may not be the best choice for neutralization. What problems may be encountered when using a strong acid for neutralizing a base? K/U

6. Why is sodium hydrogen carbonate, $NaHCO_3$, considered to be a unique neutralizing agent? K/U

7. Sodium hydroxide, NaOH, is a common base that is used in the house as a drain cleaner. K/U
   (a) Given that bases such as NaOH can be so damaging to human health, why is this base so commonly used as a drain cleaner?

   (b) In addition to containing sodium hydroxide, drain cleaners often also contain chemicals which increase the speed of the reaction. These chemicals are known as _____.

Mining, Metallurgy, and the Environment

Textbook pp. 212–217

Vocabulary

mineral	metallurgy	flash smelting
ore	smelting	

MAIN IDEA: Metals used in everyday life are important. Acquiring these metals, however, requires considerable effort. Mining and metallurgy are integral processes involved in obtaining base metals.

1. A(n) _____ is a naturally occurring solid that has a definite crystal structure and chemical composition. K/U

2. In order to access ores, mining companies can use two mining methods: _____ and _____. K/U

3. Surface mining poses unique environmental challenges. Explain why. K/U

LEARNING TIP

Base Metals
Do not let the term "base metals" confuse you. Their name has nothing to do with the bases that neutralize acids. Rather, the word "base" has a very ancient origin, and means "common" or "of little value."

4. The physical processing of ore typically includes a process known as flotation. Use **Figure 1** to describe flotation in your own words. K/U C

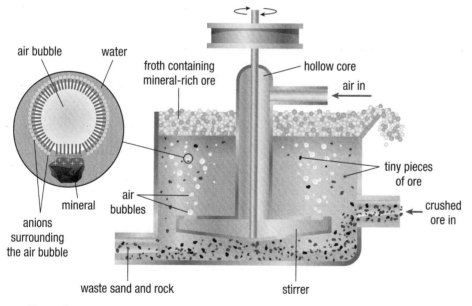

Figure 1

5. Metallurgy involves four processes. Two of these processes are physical and two are chemical. Complete the graphic organizer (**Figure 2**), noting each of the processes and providing a brief description of each. K/U C

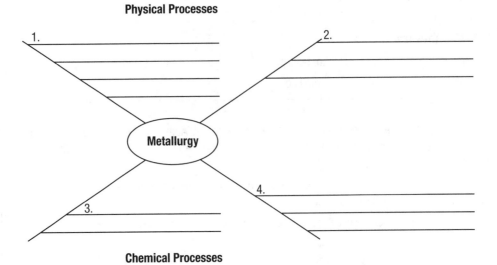

Physical Processes

1. _____

2. _____

Metallurgy

3. _____

4. _____

Chemical Processes

Figure 2

6. _____ is the chemical process that extracts a metal from its ore using heat and chemicals. K/U

7. Smelting produces sulfur dioxide gas as a by-product. K/U T/I A

    (a) What impact did this gas have on the environment?

    (b) What steps were taken to reduce sulfur dioxide gas emissions?

    (c) What other steps have been taken to reduce the emissions from the smelting process?

8. Copper obtained from the smelting process is not useful in the production of electrical equipment. T/I C A

(a) Why?

(b) **Figure 3**, below, depicts the process of electrolysis. Describe in your own words what is occurring in this process.

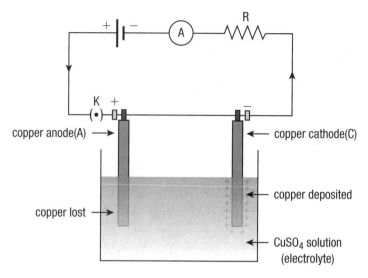

Figure 3 The electrolysis of copper

MAIN IDEA: Mining and metallurgy are processes that negatively impact the environment.

9. Discharge from metallurgical process is often acidic. K/U T/I A

(a) What substances can be used to neutralize this acidic discharge?

(b) Assuming that the acid by-products produced from the mining process are weakly acidic, would it be realistic to use a powerful base such as sodium hydroxide, NaOH, for neutralization? Why or why not?

Detox for Contaminated Land

Vocabulary

remediation   bioremediation   phytoremediation

MAIN IDEA: Contamination of the environment through the discharge of harmful chemicals has created a legacy of problems for mankind. Understanding the impacts of contaminated land is useful for motivating cleanup and remediation. Different techniques can be used for detoxification of contaminated land.

1. Contaminated land contains hazardous substances that pose a threat to human health. K/U T/I A

   (a) Describe how contaminants affect human health.

   (b) Two methods that can be used to remove contaminants from the land are _____ and _____.

   (c) What is the difference between these two methods?

   (d) Which method of contaminant removal is most effective for developing an industrial site into a parking lot? Why?

2. There are four types of remediation that can be used for detoxification of contaminated land. Complete the organizer by listing a specific technique that can be used through the identified mediation approach. K/U C

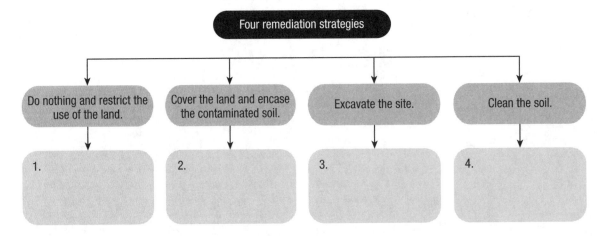

MAIN IDEA: There are three different techniques that can be used for remediation of the soil. These include physical remediation through soil flushing; chemical remediation, including stabilization and solidification, chemical oxidation, and electrolysis; and bioremediation.

3. Of the remediation strategies noted, cleaning the soil is the most complex, often requiring the use of several different techniques. K/U T/I C

(a) What occurs in the process of soil flushing?

LEARNING **TIP**

Bioremediation
"Bio" means living things. "Remediation" means "to fix." Bioremediation means using living things to fix the environment.

(b) Chemical remediation includes stabilization and solidification, chemical oxidation, and electrolysis. Explain each.

(c) Describe the process of bioremediation in your own words.

(d) What are some benefits that bioremediation offers over physical and chemical remediation?

(e) What is the principle drawback of bioremediation?

4. Phytoremediation is a type of bioremediation. Define this process in your own words. K/U C

5. What happens when a plant cannot decompose contaminants from the soil and groundwater? K/U

Green Chemistry in Industry

Textbook pp. 222–227

MAIN IDEA: Chemical processes can have negative impacts on the environment. The development of green chemistry provides a balance between the ability of chemical companies to be profitable while still protecting the environment.

1. The phrase "benign by design" is often associated with green chemistry. In your own words, what does this phrase mean in relation to green chemistry? K/U C A

2. Is the following statement true or false? If you think the statement is false, rewrite it to make it true: As a result of going green, companies have become less profitable and competitive. K/U

3. Complete **Table 1** to show some of the benefits and drawbacks of going green. K/U C

Table 1 Benefits and Drawbacks of Going Green

Benefits	Drawbacks

MAIN IDEA: Specific principles can be used to help guide the development of green chemistry.

4. Five specific principles for creating green chemistry in industry have been noted. Complete **Table 2** below, indicating the five principles that are essential to the development of green chemistry. K/U C

Table 2 The Five Principles of Green Chemistry

Principle	Concept
1	
2	
3	
4	
5	

5. _____ increase the rate of reaction, reducing the energy needed to complete a reaction. K/U
   (a) scrubbers
   (b) enzymes
   (c) catalysts
   (d) precipitates

6. How does energy reduction contribute to the development of green chemistry? K/U A

7. Applying the principles of green chemistry requires some consideration of the way in which they can be applied. **Figure 1** represents a generic industrial process. Using the principles of green chemistry and circled letters, describe how four of the principles could be applied to this process to make it a green operation. K/U T/I C A

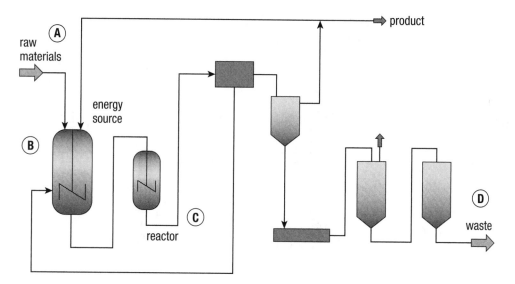

Figure 1

8. Is the following statement true or false? If you think the statement is false, rewrite it to make it true: Closed loop manufacturing involves the recycling of wastes so they are not released back into the environment. K/U

Chemical Processes

The combustion of hydrocarbons sets the stage for understanding how waste products can be produced through incomplete combustion of these materials. The waste created from these reactions has significant environmental impact. The graphic organizer summarizes some of the main ideas from Chapter 5. Fill in the blanks and add your own notes and diagrams to make study notes.

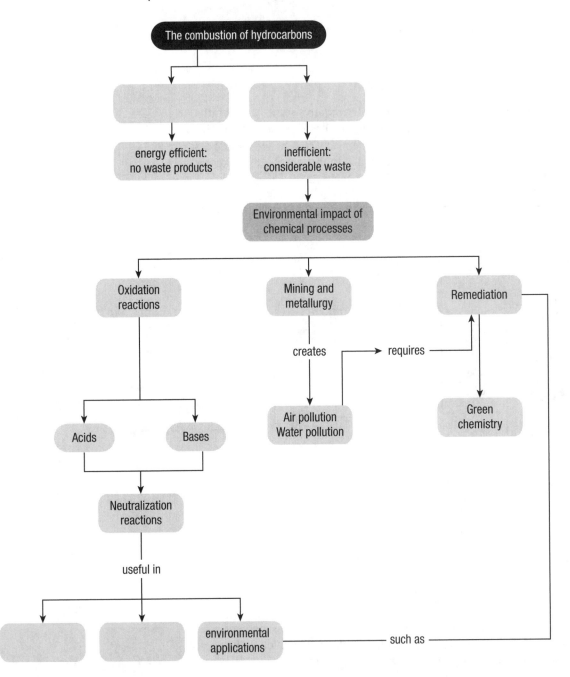

1. _____ is the science and technology of separating and refining metals from their ores and subsequent processing. (5.5) K/U

   (a) mining

   (b) ores

   (c) metallurgy

   (d) remediation

2. $H_2SO_4(aq) + CaCO_3(s) \rightarrow H_2CO_3(aq) + CaSO_4(aq)$ is an example of:

   (a) a double displacement reaction

   (b) a neutralization reaction

   (c) both a and b

   (d) a synthesis reaction (5.4) K/U

3. Are the following statements true or false? If you think the statements are false, rewrite them to make them true. K/U

   (a) The reaction below represents an example of complete combustion. (5.1)
   $$C_8H_{18} + O_2(g) \rightarrow C(s) + H_2O(l)$$

   (b) The pH of rainwater is typically 7. (5.3)

4. _____ is a chemical reaction in which fuel burns in oxygen. (5.1) K/U

5. A _____ is a reaction in which an acid reacts with a base to produce a final solution in which the pH is closer to neutral or 7.0. (5.4) K/U

6. Incomplete combustion may be harmful to the environment. Why? (5.1) T/I A

7. Consider the elements in **Table 1** below. Assuming that the elements react to form oxides, indicate whether these oxides would be acidic or basic. (5.3) K/U C

Table 1 Acidic or Basic Oxides

Element	Acidic or Basic?
carbon	
sodium	
calcium	
nitrogen	

K/U Knowledge/Understanding
T/I Thinking/Investigation
C   Communication
A   Application

8. There are three environmental hazards that can result from the metallurgy/mining industry. Complete the cause/effect graphic organizer (**Figure 1**), indicating all three hazards. (5.5) K/U C A

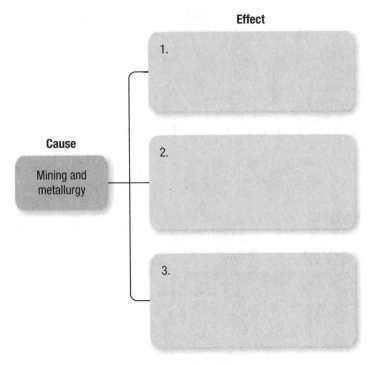

Figure 1

9. Complete the graphic organizer (**Figure 2**) below, showing the three types of remediation strategies and one example for each. (5.6) K/U C A

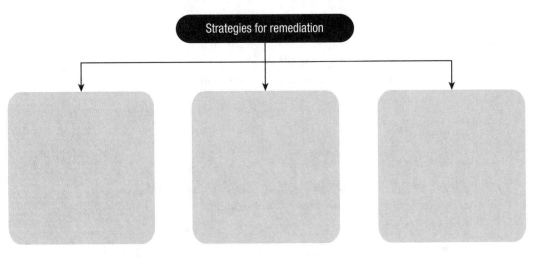

Figure 2

1. Chemical equations must be balanced because of _____. (5.1) K/U
   (a) remediation
   (b) the law of conservation
   (c) the law of decomposition
   (d) green chemistry

2. A neutralization reaction is a type of _____ reaction. (5.4) K/U
   (a) synthesis
   (b) decomposition
   (c) single displacement
   (d) double displacement

3. Is the following statement true or false? If you think the statement is false, rewrite it to make it true: Remediation of the land involves the complete removal of all of the hazardous contaminants. (5.6) K/U

4. _____ involves the burning of a hydrocarbon to produce water and carbon dioxide. (5.1) K/U
   (a) incomplete combustion
   (b) neutralization
   (c) complete combustion
   (d) green chemistry

5. _____ is a process by which minerals are removed from the ground. (5.6) K/U

6. Consider the following reaction: (4.5) K/U T/I
$$Br_2(s) + 2NaCl(aq) \rightarrow$$
   (a) Will a reaction occur?

   (b) Why or why not?

7. Metals and non-metals react to form basic and acidic oxides. Predict whether the products of the following reactions will be acidic or basic: (5.3) K/U T/I
   (a) $Na_2O + H_2O(l) \rightarrow$

   (b) $SO_2 + H_2O(l) \rightarrow$

8. Is the strongest base always the best choice for neutralizing an acid? Why or why not? (5.4) T/I A

K/U   Knowledge/Understanding
T/I   Thinking/Investigation
C   Communication
A   Application

9. Complete **Table 1** indicating the type of reaction that has occurred. Remember that each reaction may be classified under more than one reaction type. (4.2, 4.4, 4.6, 5.1, 5.3, 5.4) K/U T/I

Table 1 Reaction Types

Reaction	Type
$Cu(OH)_2 + 2\ HC_2H_3O_2 \rightarrow Cu(C_2H_3O_2)_2 + 2\ H_2O$	
$CH_4 + 2\ O_2(g) \rightarrow CO_2\ (g) + 2\ H_2O(l)$	
$4\ Fe + 3\ O_2 \rightarrow 2\ Fe_2O_3(s)$	
$Zn(s) + CuCl_2(l) \rightarrow ZnCl_2(l) + Cu(s)$	
$H_2SO_4 + 2\ NH_4OH \rightarrow (NH_4)_2SO_4 + 2\ H_2O$	
$2\ Na_2(s) + O_2(g) \rightarrow 2\ Na_2O(s)$	
$2\ HCl(l) \rightarrow H_2(g) + Cl_2(g)$	
$2\ C_8H_{18} + 17\ O_2(g) \rightarrow 16\ CO(g) + 18\ H_2O(l)$	
$Cu(s) + 2\ AgNO_3(aq) \rightarrow 2\ Ag(s) + Cu(NO_3)_2(aq)$	

10. Complete the graphic organizer (**Figure 1**) showing the five principles of green chemistry. K/U

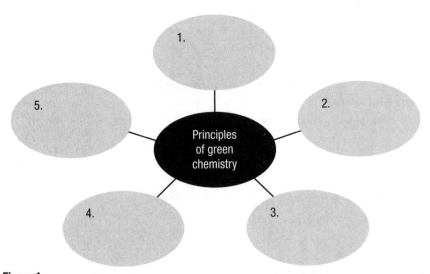

Figure 1

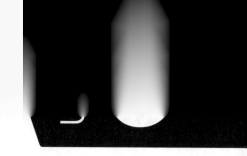

Chapter 6: Quantities in Chemical Formulas

The mole is the key to understanding both qualitative and quantitative relationships in chemical reactions. The mole represents the number of entities in a given mass of an element or compound. There are 6.02×10^{23} entities in a mole of a compound or element. This quantity is known as Avogadro's constant.

Every compound or element has its own characteristic molar mass and atomic mass. For example, the C-12 isotope of carbon collectively has a mass of exactly 12.0 g. Thus, C-12 has a molar mass, M, of 12.0 g and each carbon atom has an atomic mass of 12.0 u. The concept of the mole can be extended to calculate the mass (m) or the number of entities (N) that participate in chemical reactions. From there, the empirical formula (the simplest whole number formula ratio) and the chemical formula (the actual number of atoms in a single molecule of a molecular compound) can also be determined. Since all forms of matter follow the law of definite proportions, these concepts can finally be extended to calculating the percentage composition of a compound by the mass of its constituent components.

Chapter 7: Stoichiometry in Chemical Reactions

In any reaction, $A + B \rightarrow AB$, the stoichiometric amount of each reagent, is the amount that will completely react without any reactant being left over once the reaction is complete. A stoichiometric reaction is an "ideal" reaction. Spillage, impurities, side reactions, and other factors render most real-world reactions less than stoichiometric. In the real world, chemists usually do not attempt to assemble stoichiometric amounts of reagents. Instead, in a reaction like the one given above, chemists deliberately measure out an excess amount of one reactant, thus conferring the other reactant with the status of limiting reactant. In most real-world reactions, the limiting reactant is the component that determines the theoretical yield of the reaction under ideal conditions. This theoretical yield is compared to the actual measured yield in the laboratory, allowing the percentage yield to be calculated as a measure of how efficient the reaction was.

BIG IDEAS

- Relationships in chemical reactions can be described quantitatively.
- The efficiency of chemical reactions can be determined and optimized by applying an understanding of quantitative relationships in such reactions.

Qualitative and Quantitative Analysis

Textbook pp. 260–263

> **Vocabulary**
>
> qualitative analysis   quantitative analysis

MAIN IDEA: Qualitative analysis involves identification of properties and characteristics while quantitative analysis involves collection of numerical data.

1. Is the following statement true or false? If you think the statement is false, rewrite it to make it true: Determining the proper dosage of medicine for a patient is a matter of qualitative analysis for a doctor. K/U

2. The following four factors influence the health of a person with diabetes. Which factor is qualitative? K/U
   (a) the patient's range of glucose concentration in the blood
   (b) the patient's level of insulin in the blood after eating
   (c) what kinds of exercises the patient does regularly
   (d) the patient's basal metabolic rate as measured by calories burned per hour

3. Read the questions in **Table 1**. Determine whether each question is asking primarily for a qualitative or quantitative analysis. Place a check mark in the appropriate column. T/I

Table 1 Qualitative and Quantitative Questions

Questions	Qualitative	Quantitative
Is the solution an acid or a base?		
What is the pH of the solution?		
Does the patient have sugar in his blood?		
At what temperature does sugar melt?		
What concentration of sugar does the patient have in his blood?		
Does the lake contain pollutants called PCBs?		
Is the baseball player using performance-enhancing substances?		
What dose of anabolic steroids does an athlete take to improve performance?		
Is sugar more soluble in hot water or cold water?		

4. A team of scientists is performing an analysis of high quality chocolate both qualitatively and quantitatively. List at least three pieces of information in each column of **Table 2** that you think the scientists would analyze. ◼A

Table 2 Qualitative and Quantitative Analysis of Chocolate

Qualitative analysis	Quantitative analysis

5. Which of the following measurements is both qualitative and quantitative? ◼T/I
   (a) measuring the level of carbon dioxide in a room in parts per billion
   (b) measuring whether persistent organic pollutants (POPs) are present in a pond
   (c) measuring whether persistent organic pollutants (POPs) exceed a threshold level
   (d) measuring whether a chemical reaction gives off carbon dioxide as a product

6. Identify each of the following as either qualitative or quantitative information. If the description is qualitative, write a second description that is quantitative. If the description is quantitative, write a second description that is qualitative. ◼K/U ◼C
   (a) The alligator was 3.1 m in length.

   (b) The reaction of zinc and hydrochloric acid yielded hydrogen gas.

   (c) A total of 20 g of fat contains 180 calories, but consuming it does not promote insulin release so it does not contribute to diabetes.

Textbook pp. 264–265

Overdosing on Salt

MAIN IDEA: Dietary consumption of sodium chloride creates a major health problem for Canadians.

1. Is the following statement true or false? If you think the statement is false, rewrite it to make it true: The amount of salt the average Canadian consumes is approximately equal to Health Canada's recommended daily intake. K/U

2. The harm caused by ingestion of too much salt is a complex sequence of events. Number the events from 1 to 7 to show the correct order. K/U

    ___ Sodium ion levels in the blood rise to high levels.

    ___ A person consumes too much sodium chloride in his or her diet.

    ___ Extra fluid retention swells blood vessels and increases blood pressure.

    ___ Elevated blood pressure makes the heart work harder.

    ___ Strain may damage the heart and cause cardiovascular disease.

    ___ Sodium chloride ionizes in the blood after consumption.

    ___ High sodium levels cause the body to retain excess water.

3. In order to get to the recommended daily intake of sodium, by how much would the average Canadian need to cut his or her salt consumption? T/I

4. Randy consumes about 2500 mg of sodium each day. T/I C A

    (a) How does Randy's consumption compare to the typical Canadian? Is Randy's diet healthy? Explain.

    (b) If Randy stops using table salt, will his diet be healthy? Explain.

5. Complete **Table 1** to identify high-sodium foods and alternatives that are lower in sodium. K/U A

    Table 1 High-Sodium Foods and Low-Sodium Alternatives

Type of food	High-sodium food	Low-sodium alternative
meat		
cheese		
fish		
vegetable		
snack		

The Mole—A Unit of Counting

Vocabulary		
mole	Avogadro's constant (N_A)	amount (n)

Textbook pp. 266–270

MAIN IDEA: You can estimate the number of identical items in a large group as long as the mass of an item is known and the mass of the entire group is known.

1. You can calculate the quantity of entities in a large group by _____ the mass of the group by the mass of _____. **K/U**

2. Is the following statement true or false? If you think the statement is false, rewrite it to make it true: The only way to get a precise count of the number of entities in a large group is to count them individually. **K/U**

> **LEARNING TIP**
>
> **Entity**
> The word "entity" is a general term used to refer to particles of matter. Atoms, molecules, and ions are all entities that make up matter.

3. A chemist writes the equation $H_2(g) + Cl_2(g) \rightarrow 2\ HCl(g)$. What is she indicating? **K/U**

   (a) Each molecule of H_2 in the sample reacts with each molecule of Cl_2 to produce 2 molecules of HCl.

   (b) A single molecule of H_2 in the sample reacts with a single molecule of Cl_2 to produce a single molecule of HCl.

   (c) Molecules of H_2 react with molecules of Cl_2 in a 1:1 ratio to produce HCl molecules in a 2:1 ratio with each of the reactants.

   (d) Two molecules of hydrogen react with 2 molecules of chlorine to produce 2 molecules of hydrochloric acid.

4. You have several different bags full of metal nuts and bolts. You want to use mass measurements to estimate the number of entities in each bag. Fill in **Table 1** below to evaluate how accurate your estimate would be in each case. Explain your decisions. **T/I C A**

Table 1 Accuracy of Estimation Using Mass

What you are measuring	What you know	Accuracy of estimate	Explanation
bolts	• mass of each bolt • total mass		
nuts and bolts	• mass of each bolt • mass of each nut • total mass		
small- and large-sized bolts	• mass of each bolt • total mass		
equal quantities of nuts and bolts	• mass of each bolt • mass of each nut • total mass		
bolts	• mass of each bolt		

5. Ten-penny nails have a mass of 14.1 g each. A bag of nails has a mass of 7.13 kg. How many nails are in the bag? T/I

6. Three boxes are filled to the top with different proportions of nuts and bolts (Figure 1). T/I C A

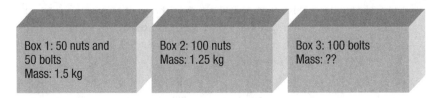

Figure 1

(a) Which item has a greater mass, a nut or a bolt? Explain how you know.

(b) How would the mass of Box 3 compare to Box 2? Explain how you know.

(c) How would the mass of Box 3 compare to Box 1? Explain how you know.

MAIN IDEA: A mole is a counting unit that is used to quantify atoms, molecules, and other entities that exist in extremely large quantities.

7. Compare the three items listed below. T/I A
   - a mole of atoms
   - a mole of golf balls
   - a mole of bowling balls

   (a) Which of the three would have the greatest number of items? Explain how you know.

   (b) How many atoms are there? golf balls? bowling balls?

8. Is the following statement true or false? If you think the statement is false, rewrite it to make it true: A mole is the number of carbon atoms in exactly 12 g of a typical sample of pure carbon. K/U

9. Mark each number below as greater, less than, or equal to Avogadro's number. T/I A

   (a) 6.02×10^{24} is _____ Avogadro's number.
   (b) 9 000 000 000 000 000 000 000 is _____ Avogadro's number.
   (c) 6.02×10^{22} is _____ Avogadro's number.
   (d) 602 000 000 000 000 000 000 000 is _____ Avogadro's number.
   (e) 10^{22} is _____ Avogadro's number.
   (f) 7×10^{22} is _____ Avogadro's number.

10. How many entities does half a mole contain? T/I

    (a) 3.01×10^{11}
    (b) 3.01×10^{12}
    (c) $6.02 \times 10^{11.5}$
    (d) 3.01×10^{23}

11. Match each number on the left to the equivalent number on the right. T/I

    (a) 6.02×10^{23} (i) 0.602×10^{23}
    (b) 2.5×10^{2} (ii) 2.5
    (c) 25×10^{-3} (iii) 0.25
    (d) 250×10^{-2} (iv) 2500
    (e) 0.25×10^{0} (v) 2.5×10^{-2}
    (f) 250×10^{1} (vi) 60.2×10^{22}
    (g) 6.02×10^{22} (vii) 250

12. Calculate each answer. T/I

    (a) $(4.2 \times 10^{-4})(6 \times 10^{7})$

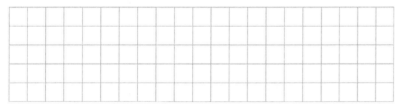

    (b) $(5.756 \times 10^{1}) + (4.200 \times 10^{-1})$

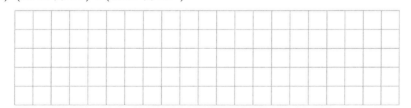

    (c) $(1.8 \times 10^{-6}) \div (3 \times 10^{-5})$

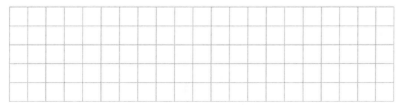

LEARNING TIP

Scientific Notation
You will use scientific notation frequently in this unit. For a quick refresher on how to use scientific notation correctly, refer to Skills Handbook section A6.1 in your textbook.

STUDY TIP

Exponent Rules
Remember to add exponents when you multiply in scientific notation, and subtract exponents when you divide. When dividing, keep in mind that subtracting a negative is equivalent to adding a positive.

Molar Mass

> **Vocabulary**
>
> molar mass

MAIN IDEA: A molar mass, *M*, is the mass of one mole of a pure substance, an element, or compound.

1. Is the following statement true or false? If you think the statement is false, rewrite it to make it true: For all molecular elements, molar mass and atomic mass have the same value. K/U

2. The mass of 1 mole of a compound is 48.55 g. What is the mass of 1 molecule of the same compound? K/U

3. To calculate the molar mass of the ionic compound sodium hydroxide, NaOH, which of the following do you need to calculate? K/U
   (a) the formula unit
   (b) the molecular formula
   (c) both the formula unit and the molecular formula
   (d) the molecular formula for each ion

MAIN IDEA: The molar mass of a compound can be determined by calculating the sum of each entity in a compound.

4. Calculate the molar mass of the following molecular compounds. T/I
   (a) sulfur dioxide, SO_2

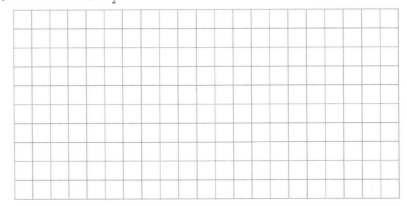

   (b) ethanol, C_2H_5OH

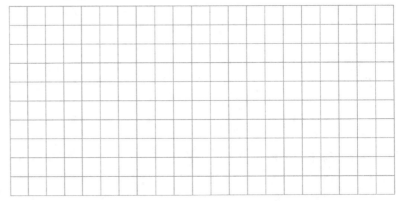

5. Calculate the molar mass of the following ionic compounds. T/I
   (a) calcium chloride, $CaCl_2$

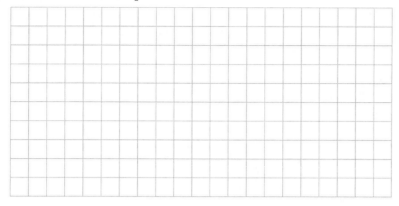

LEARNING **TIP**

Periodic Table
You will refer to the periodic table frequently in this Chemistry course. The periodic table is provided on the inside back cover of your textbook and in Appendix B1.

   (b) iron(III) nitrate, $Fe(NO_3)_3$

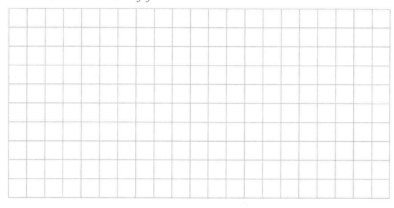

MAIN IDEA: Molar mass helps you convert a mass of a pure substance to moles and vice versa.

6. Which equation will tell you how the mass of a sample in grams is related to the amount of the substance in moles? Explain. K/U C

7. A compound has a molar mass of 50 g. You have 200 g of the compound. How many moles of the compound do you have? K/U T/I
   (a) 0.25
   (b) 4
   (c) 150
   (d) cannot be determined

8. For soiled clothes, a manufacturer recommends adding 60.0 g of bleach, NaClO, to laundry. How many moles of bleach is this? T/I

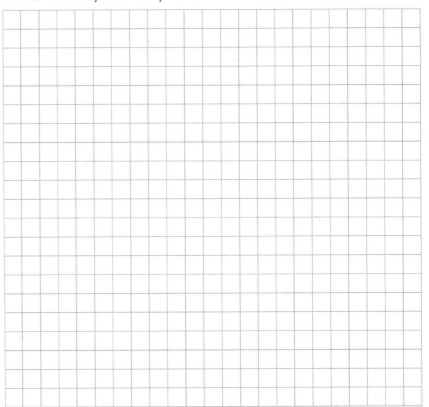

9. The average person exhales about 900 g of carbon dioxide, CO_2, each day. How many moles does a person exhale in one hour? T/I

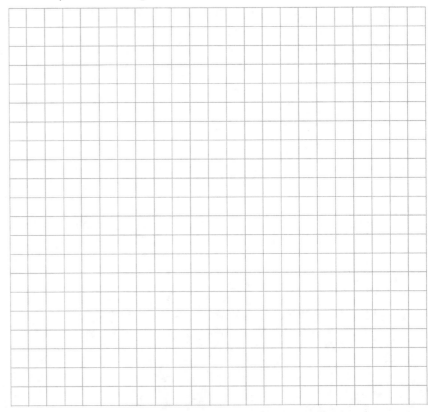

Mass and Number of Entities

MAIN IDEA: The number of entities in a sample, N, is determined by multiplying the amount of the substance in moles, n, by Avogadro's constant, N_A:

Textbook pp. 278–283

$N = nN_A$

1. The number of entities in 1 mole of a substance is equal to _____. K/U

2. (a) Will a 10 g sample of gold and a 10 g sample of silver have the same number of atoms? Explain.

   (b) Which sample will have more atoms? Explain how you know. K/U A

3. Which expression shows how to calculate the number of days in 11 weeks? K/U T/I

   (a) $(11 \text{ weeks}) \times \left(\dfrac{1 \text{ week}}{7 \text{ days}} \right)$

   (b) $(11 \text{ weeks}) \div \left(\dfrac{7 \text{ days}}{1 \text{ week}} \right)$

   (c) $\left(\dfrac{7 \text{ days}}{1 \text{ week}} \right) \div (11 \text{ weeks})$

   (d) $(11 \text{ weeks}) \times \left(\dfrac{7 \text{ days}}{1 \text{ week}} \right)$

4. Fill in **Table 1** to compare how you can count the number of entities in a group if you know the number of entities in the group and the number of groups. Some of the categories have been filled in for you. K/U T/I A

   Table 1 Properties of Elements

Entity name	Cupcakes	Days	Minutes	Atoms
Entity variable	*cups*	*day*	*min*	*N*
Group name	dozen	week	hours	mole
Group variable				
Group amount				
Number of groups	*n*	*n*	*n*	*n*
Number of items: equation				
Number of items for *n* = 5				

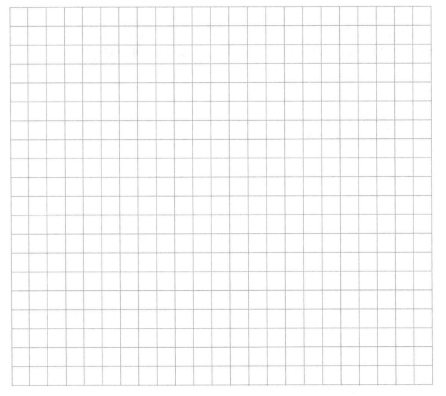

LEARNING TIP

When to Round Off Answers
Whenever the answer to one calculation will be used in a later calculation, rounding off early introduces unnecessary errors in the answer. Always round off after the last calculation.

5. An MP3 player case is made of plastic and aluminum. The aluminum part of the case has a mass of 80.00 g. Calculate the number of atoms in this 80.00 g sample of aluminum. T/I

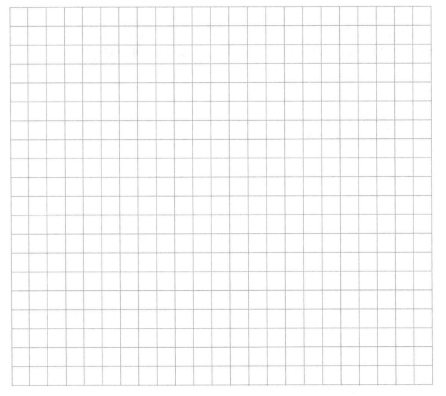

STUDY TIP

Check Your Units
When solving problems, always write the units in your terms, and cancel the units just like fractional numbers. When you reach your solution, always check to make sure that your units are correct.

6. Carbon tetrachloride, CCl_4, was widely used as a refrigerant and in fire extinguishers until it was determined to be harmful to the environment. A fire extinguisher shoots out 1.50 kg of carbon tetrachloride. How many molecules of this compound were released? T/I

7. A spacecraft took a 5.0 g sample of sulfuric acid, H_2SO_4, from the planet Venus. T/I

(a) How many molecules of H_2SO_4 did this sample include?

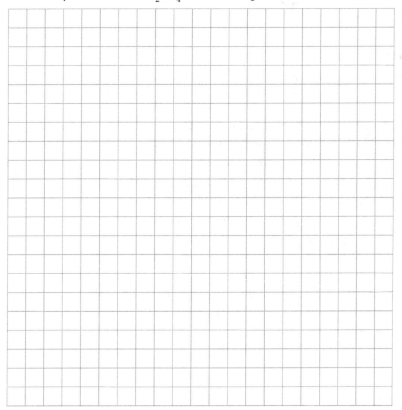

(b) How many atoms of hydrogen, sulfur, and oxygen did this sample of H_2SO_4 include?

6.5 Mass and Number of Entities

The Composition of Unknown Compounds

Textbook pp. 284–288

Vocabulary

percentage composition   law of definite proportions

MAIN IDEA: Percentage composition determines the proportion of each element in a compound by mass, not by relative number of entities.

1. In combustion of hydrocarbons, a hydrocarbon with the general formula $C_xH_yO_z$ produces oxygen, _____ and _____. K/U

2. Combustion analysis helps a chemist determine which of the following? K/U
   (a) the percentage of each type of atom in a compound
   (b) the percentage of carbon dioxide in a compound
   (c) the percentage of carbon and hydrogen in a compound
   (d) the molar ratio of water to carbon dioxide in a compound

3. Is the following statement true or false? If you think the statement is false, rewrite it to make it true: The law of definite proportions states that if you break down any quantity of a compound, it always will yield the same percentage composition by mass. K/U

4. **Table 1** shows the combustion of an unknown compound with the formula $C_xH_yO_z$. T/I C A
   (a) Fill in the missing values in the table.

Table 1 Combustion Analysis of $C_xH_yO_z$

Sample number	Mass of compound (g)	Mass of carbon (g)	Mass of hydrogen (g)	Mass of oxygen (g)
1	20.00	10.44	2.60	6.96
2	30.00	15.66	3.90	10.44
3	40.00			
4	50.00			

   (b) Explain how the values you provided in the table are consistent with the law of definite proportions.

5. **Table 2** shows the combustion of unknown compounds with the formula $C_xH_yO_z$. T/I C A

Table 2 Combustion Analysis of $C_xH_yO_z$

Sample number	Mass of compound (g)	Mass of carbon (g)	Mass of hydrogen (g)	Mass of oxygen (g)
1	10.00	5.22	1.30	3.48
2	10.00	3.87	0.97	5.16
3	15.00	5.80	1.46	7.74
4	15.00	7.83	1.95	5.22

(a) Compare Sample 1 to Sample 2. If the two are consistent with the law of definite proportions, how do you explain this data?

(b) Which other sample in the table is the same compound as Sample 1? How do you know?

(c) Which other sample in the table is the same compound as Sample 2? How do you know?

6. When disturbed, bombardier beetles shoot out a noxious spray that includes hydroquinone, $C_6H_6O_2$. An 82.59 g sample of hydroquinone contains 24.00 g of oxygen and 4.55 g of hydrogen. If the rest of the mass of the compound is carbon, what is the percentage composition of hydroquinone? T/I

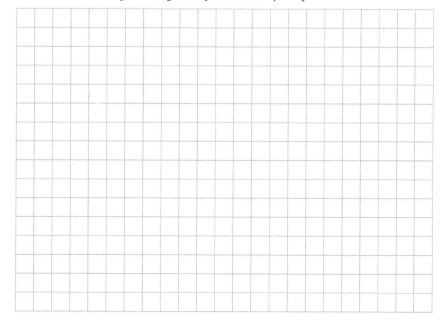

7. Calculate the percentage composition of potassium sulfate, K_2SO_4. T/I

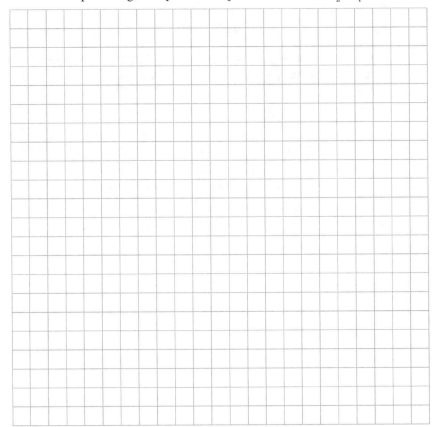

8. A single glucose molecule has the formula $C_6H_{12}O_6$. A hexane, a simple six-carbon hydrocarbon, has the formula C_6H_{14}. In which compound does carbon make up a greater proportion of the total composition? T/I

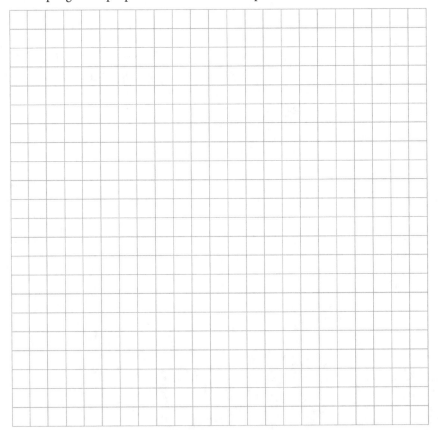

Empirical Formulas

Vocabulary

empirical formula   molecular formula

Textbook pp. 289–293

MAIN IDEA: The empirical formula identifies the simplest whole number ratio of elements in a compound. The molecular formula identifies the actual number of atoms in a molecule.

1. The empirical formula for the compound hydrogen peroxide, H_2O_2, is which of the following? **K/U**
   - (a) HO
   - (b) H_2O
   - (c) H_2O_2
   - (d) 2 [HO]

LEARNING **TIP**

Determining Ratios
One way to determine the ratios of entities is to divide each amount by the smallest amount. The smallest amount becomes "1." The other amounts have higher values, relative to 1.

2. Is the following statement true or false? If you think the statement is false, rewrite it to make it true: Two compounds with the same empirical formula can have very different properties but they must share the same molar mass. **K/U**

3. Which of the following statements is true? **K/U**
   - (a) The number of atoms in an empirical formula is always less than the number of atoms in a molecular formula.
   - (b) The number of atoms in an empirical formula is always greater than the number of atoms in a molecular formula.
   - (c) The number of atoms in an empirical formula can be greater than or equal to the number of atoms in a molecular formula.
   - (d) The number of atoms in an empirical formula can be less than or equal to the number of atoms in a molecular formula.

LEARNING **TIP**

An Analogy for Empirical Formula
Imagine a "compound" that contains exactly 2 thumbs, T, and 8 fingers, F. The molecular formula for this compound is T_2F_8. Since there is 1 thumb for every 4 fingers, the simplest ratio of thumbs to fingers is 1:4. Therefore, the empirical formula of this compound is TF_4.

4. Write the empirical formula and the molecular formula for each of the following compounds. **T/I C**

   (a)   H—O H
         | |
      H—C—C—H
         | |
         H—O H

      empirical formula:
      molecular formula:

   (c)   H
              |
         H—C—O—H
              |
         H—O

      empirical formula:
      molecular formula:

   (b)   H—O H
         | |
      H—C—C=O
         |
         H—O

      empirical formula:
      molecular formula:

   (d) H—O   O—H
        | |
     H—C—C=O
        |
        H—O

      empirical formula:
      molecular formula:

Molecular formula: T_2F_8
Empirical formula: TF_4

6.7 Empirical Formulas   **105**

5. An ionic compound contains 75.5 % copper, Cu, by mass and 24.5 % phosphorus, P. Determine the empirical formula for the compound. T/I

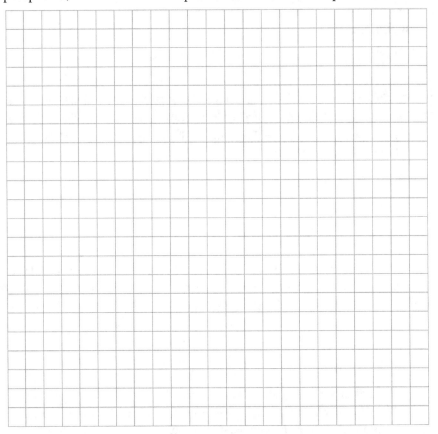

6. Silicic acid contains 2.6 % hydrogen, H, by mass, 36.0 % silicon, Si, and 61.5 % oxygen, O. Determine the empirical formula for the compound. T/I

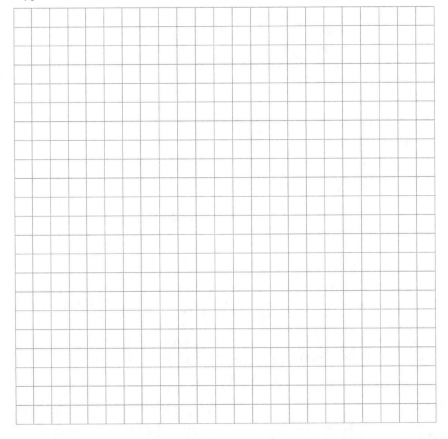

Chemistry JOURNAL

Drug-Contaminated Currency

Textbook pp. 294–295

MAIN IDEA: Scientists ran an experiment to determine whether money-counting machines were responsible for contaminating British banknotes with cocaine.

1. Classify the experiment described in this Chemistry Journal as a controlled experiment, a correlational study, or a field study. Explain your thinking. T/I C A

2. Is the following statement true or false? If you think the statement is false, rewrite it to make it true: The data collected in this experiment shows that money-counting machines are fully responsible for the contamination of British currency with cocaine. K/U

3. Write a hypothesis for the experiment conducted by the researchers at the University of Bristol. C A

4. If their hypothesis was correct, what would the researchers at the University of Bristol have expected to find? K/U A
   (a) At least some of the slips of paper became contaminated from the machines.
   (b) All of the slips of paper became contaminated from the machines.
   (c) All of the banknotes became contaminated from the machines.
   (d) More slips of paper became contaminated than banknotes.

5. Complete **Table 1** to summarize the process of identifying the compounds on the strips of paper. K/U

Table 1 Desorption and Mass Spectrometer Analysis

Step	What happens	Purpose
Thermal desorption		
Mass spectrometer ionization		
Mass spectrometer deflection		
Mass spectrometer spectrum		

6. What conclusions do you draw from the data collected in this experiment? Explain. T/I A

Molecular Formulas

Textbook pp. 296–300

MAIN IDEA: The molecular formula is always a whole-number multiple of the empirical formula, and empirical and molecular formulas can be the same.

1. Volatile organic compounds, VOCs, can be synthetic or _____ and consist primarily of _____ and _____. K/U

2. Is the following statement true or false? If you think the statement is false, rewrite it to make it true: If you know the empirical formula for a compound, you can always figure out the compound's chemical formula. K/U

Use **Figure 1** to answer Questions 3 to 5.

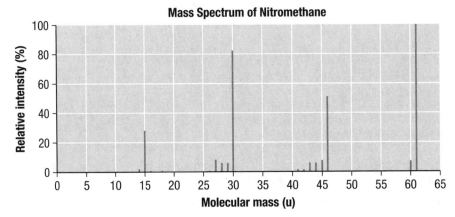

Figure 1

3. What is the most likely molecular mass of nitromethane? How do you know? T/I

4. Which of the following most likely identifies the chemical formula for nitromethane? T/I
   (a) HNO_3
   (b) CH_3NO_2
   (c) C_3H_7OH
   (d) $CH_3N(OH)_2$

5. What is the largest fragment with a molecular mass of 30 likely to be? Explain how you know. T/I

6. Ribose is a compound that makes up the backbone of DNA, the genetic material. Ribose has an empirical formula of CH_2O and a molar mass of 150.13 g/mol. Determine the molecular formula for ribose. T/I

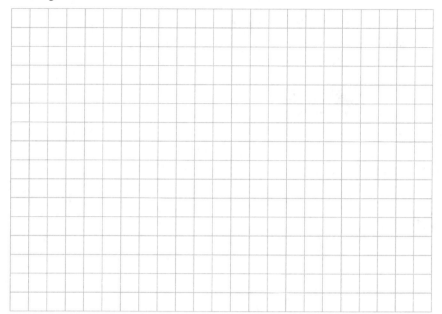

7. A compound is 53.3 % carbon, 11.2 % hydrogen, and 35.5 % oxygen, and has a molar mass of 90.14 g/mol. Determine the molecular formula for the compound. T/I

Quantities in Chemical Formulas

This graphic organizer presents the main ideas from Chapter 6. You can use this map to review the chapter and solidify your understanding of the concepts it presents.

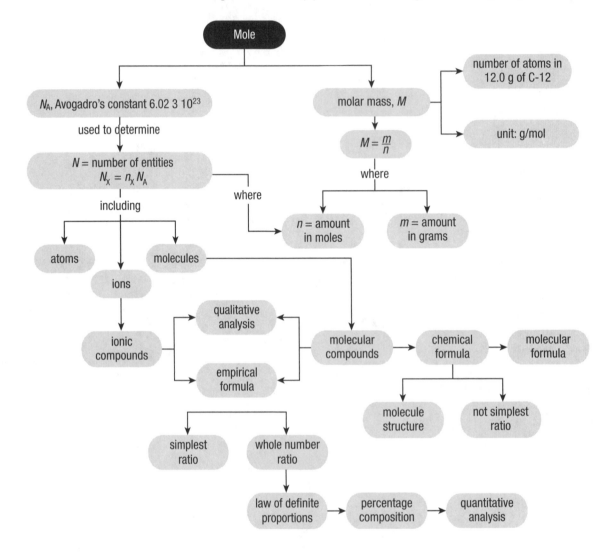

1. Identify each of the following as qualitative or quantitative information. If the description is qualitative, write a second description that is quantitative. If the description is quantitative, write a second description that is qualitative. (6.1) K/U C A

   (a) The patient's blood sugar was 7.0 mmol/L.

   (b) A small sample of glucose will dissolve in warm water.

   K/U Knowledge/Understanding
   T/I Thinking/Investigation
   C   Communication
   A   Application

2. Is the following statement true or false? If you think the statement is false, rewrite it to make it true: Most of the excess salt in the average Canadian's diet comes from pouring too much salt on fresh foods. (6.2) K/U

3. Sort the following quantities into **Figure 1**. (6.3) T/I A

   88.6×10^{22} atoms 0.06×10^{27} atoms 6.02×10^{23} bowling balls
   0.0062×10^{26} atoms   602 000 $\times 10^{18}$ pickles $1000 \times 6.2 \times 10^{20}$ pins
   99×10^{22} cookies $(13 \times 10^{10})^2$ pizzas $(5 \times 10^{12})^2$ tortilla chips
   1×10^{24} cookies $100 \times 6.02 \times 10^{21}$ pins
   700 000 000 000 000 000 molecules   590 000 $\times 10^{18}$ Ping-Pong balls

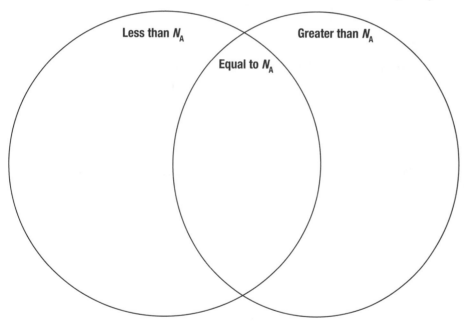

Figure 1

4. **Figure 2** shows five different quantities of matter. In the blank spaces below, rank the quantities by mass from greatest to least. (6.4) A T/I

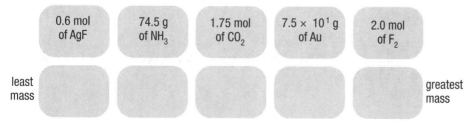

Figure 2

5. A nugget made of pure gold has a mass of 75.4 g. A pure silver nugget has a mass of 60.2 g. (6.5) T/I
   (a) Which nugget has more atoms? _____
   (b) How many more atoms does this nugget have? _____

6. **Figure 3** shows six samples of unknown compounds with the formula $C_xH_yO_z$. (6.6) T/I

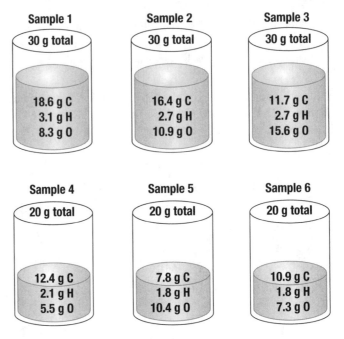

Figure 3

(a) Which sample contains the same compound as Sample 1? Explain.

(b) Which other containers contain the same compound? Explain.

7. (a) Determine the empirical formula for Sample 1 in Figure 3. (6.7) T/I

   (b) Which sample or samples in Figure 3 has the greatest percentage composition of oxygen? What is the empirical formula of this sample? (6.7) T/I

8. A compound is 60.9 % carbon, 4.4 % hydrogen, and 34.8 % oxygen, and has a molar mass of 138.1 g/mol. Determine the molecular formula for this compound. (6.9) T/I

Mole Ratios in Chemical Equations

Vocabulary

mole ratio

Textbook pp. 316–320

MAIN IDEA: A mole ratio in an equation can be used to determine the amount of product or reactant needed in a chemical reaction.

1. In the equation $4 Al(s) + 3 O_2(g) \rightarrow 2 Al_2O_3(s)$, there is a ratio of _____ between the amount of oxygen used and the amount of aluminum(III) oxide produced. K/U

2. Is the following statement true or false? If you think the statement is false, rewrite it to make it true: The total number of moles on the left side of a chemical equation always equals the total number of moles on the right side of the equation. K/U

3. Consider the reaction $2 H_2 + O_2 \rightarrow 2 H_2O$. If there is more than 1 mole of O_2 for every 2 moles of H_2, what is the result? K/U A
   (a) All of the oxygen is used, and some of the hydrogen is not used.
   (b) The number of moles of hydrogen used up is more than the number of moles of water produced as a product.
   (c) The same amount of water will be produced, but some of the oxygen will not be used.
   (d) The reaction will not occur.

4. An equation for making Buffalo wing sauce is given as follows:

   $$6 B + 4 R + 4 K + 1 H \rightarrow 1 Bf$$

   B stands for butter, R for red pepper sauce, K for ketchup, H for honey, and Bf for the product, Buffalo wing sauce. K/U T/I A
   (a) Use the equation to complete **Table 1**.

   Table 1 Buffalo Wing Synthesis

6 B +	4 R +	4 K +	1 H →	1 Bf
B	**R**	**K**	**H**	**Bf**
6				
9				
90				
$6 \times 6.02 \times 10^{23}$ = 6 mol				

   (b) Are the number of entities on both sides of the equation equal? Why or why not?

   (c) If you measured the total mass of the reactants in the equation and compared it to the mass of the product, what would you find?

5. Chlorine is prepared by combining manganese dioxide, MnO_2, with hydrochloric acid, HCl, to produce manganese chloride, $MnCl_2$, chlorine gas, Cl_2, and water. How much HCl will be needed to produce 3.25 mol of water? T/I A

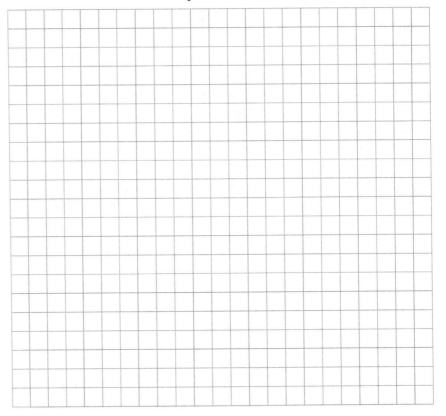

6. Nitrous acid, HNO_2, will decompose to nitric acid, HNO_3 plus water and nitric oxide, NO. What amount of nitrous acid will be needed to produce 2.5×10^{-1} mol of NO? T/I

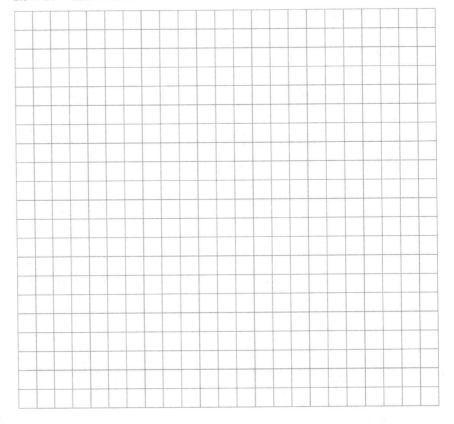

Mass Relationships in Chemical Equations

Textbook pp. 321–325

Vocabulary

stoichiometry   stoichiometric amount

MAIN IDEA: Stoichiometry involves using mole ratios in balanced equations to predict the mass amounts of products and reactants that are used in a chemical reaction.

1. The amount of a substance in moles, n, can be determined by dividing the _____ of the substance by its _____. K/U

2. In the equation $CO_2(g) + 2 LiOH(s) \rightarrow Li_2CO_3(aq) + H_2O(l)$, the stoichiometric relationship of lithium hydroxide to carbon dioxide tells us that _____ of LiOH are needed to react with _____ of CO_2. K/U

3. Is the following statement true or false? If you think the statement is false, rewrite it to make it true: If you use a stoichiometric amount of each reagent in a reaction, there will be no reactants left over when the reaction is complete. K/U

4. You are given the equation $A + B \rightarrow C$ and told that you have m grams of reactant A, or m_A. How can you find out how many grams of B, m_B, you will need to carry out the reaction? Fill in the flow chart below to outline the process (**Figure 1**).

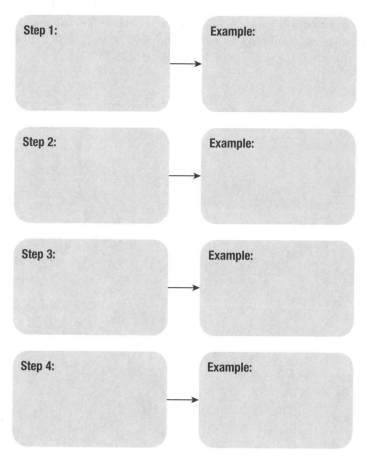

Step 1:	Example:
Step 2:	Example:
Step 3:	Example:
Step 4:	Example:

Figure 1

5. The first reaction in the production of nitric acid involves reacting ammonia, NH_3, with oxygen at high temperature according to the equation, $4 NH_3(g) + 5 O_2(g) \rightarrow 4 NO(g) + 6 H_2O$, to form nitrogen monoxide, NO. How much ammonia is required to react with 148.0 g of oxygen?

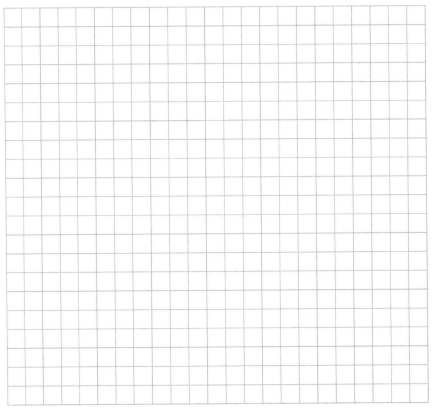

6. The equation, $I_2(s) + F_2(g) \rightarrow IF_3(s)$ shows that iodine will react with fluorine under special conditions to produce iodine[III] fluoride, IF_3. How much fluorine gas is required to produce 400.0 g of IF_3? T/I A

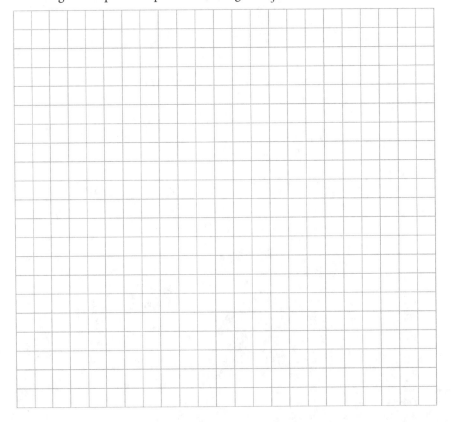

Which Reagent Runs Out First?

Vocabulary

limiting reagent

excess reagent

Textbook pp. 326–330

MAIN IDEA: The limiting reagent is the reactant that is in shorter supply and gets completely used up first. Excess reagents are reactants that remain after the reaction is complete.

1. Is the following statement true or false? If you think the statement is false, rewrite it to make it true: The compound or element that is greater in terms of molar amount is the excess reagent in a reaction. K/U

2. You add two reagents, A and B, in non-stoichiometric proportions to produce C according to the reaction A + B → C. After the reaction is complete, how can you identify the limiting reagent? K/U
    (a) It is the reagent among the products that is largest in quantity.
    (b) It is the reagent among the products that is smallest in quantity
    (c) It is the new reagent that appears among the products.
    (d) It is the reagent that no longer can be detected among the products.

3. A salad dressing recipe calls for 2 parts olive oil to be combined with 1 part vinegar. T/I A
    (a) A chef has 100 mL of olive oil and 60 mL of vinegar. Which reagent (ingredient) is the limiting reagent? Which reagent is the excess reagent?

> **STUDY TIP**
>
> **Identifying the Limiting Reagent**
> When identifying the limiting reagent, think of a peanut butter and jelly sandwich. When making the sandwich, which ingredient will you run out of first? That ingredient is the limiting reagent. For example, with a large jar of peanut butter and a small jar of jelly, you are likely to run out of jelly first, so that is the limiting reagent.

(b) What is the maximum amount of properly proportioned salad dressing that the chef can make?

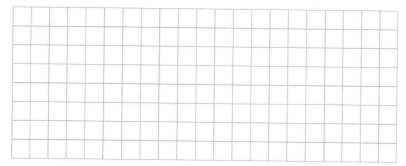

(c) How much of the excess reagent will be left over?

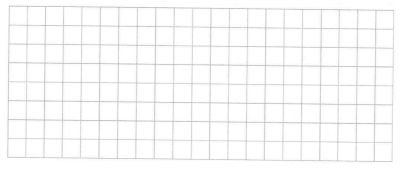

(d) How much of the limiting reagent would you need to add to cause the limiting reagent to become the excess reagent and vice versa?

4. A company combines two reagents, X and Y, according to the reaction X + Y → Z, to produce Z. Reagent X is inexpensive. Reagent Y is very expensive. Which reagent should the company use as the excess reagent? K/U

   (a) reagent X   (c) reagent Z

   (b) reagent Y   (d) There will be no excess reagent.

5. The equation for the complete combustion of gasoline (heptane) is $C_7H_{16}(g) + 11\ O_2(g) \rightarrow 7\ CO_2(g) + 8\ H_2O(g)$. Fill in **Table 1** that shows mass quantities for different quantities of reactants in this reaction. T/I A

Table 1 Combustion of Gasoline: $C_7H_{16}(g) + 11\ O_2(g) \rightarrow 7\ CO_2(g) + 8\ H_2O(g)$

Amount of C_7H_{16} (mol)	Amount of O_2 (mol)	mole ratio $n_{O_2}:n_{C_7H_{16}}$	Complete combustion?	Excess reagent
5	5			
7	56			
3×10^{-2}	5×10^{-1}			
2.3×10^3	9.2×10^2			

6. Equations for the complete and incomplete combustion of propane are:

   complete: $C_3H_8(g) + 5\ O_2(g) \rightarrow 3\ CO_2(g) + 4\ H_2O(g)$

   incomplete: $2\ C_3H_8(g) + 7\ O_2(g) \rightarrow 2\ C(s) + 2\ CO(g) + 2\ CO_2(g) + 8\ H_2O(g)$

   (a) Which type of combustion produces more carbon air pollutants, such as carbon monoxide, CO, or soot (carbon)?

   (b) Which type of combustion produces more carbon dioxide (the primary greenhouse gas) pollution? Explain your answer. T/I

MAIN IDEA: Controlling the limiting and excess reagents in a chemical reaction has important consumer, health, and environmental applications.

7. An acid spill in a pond needs to be cleaned up with a base. K/U C A

   (a) Which chemical should be considered the limiting reagent in this situation? the excess reagent?

   (b) Why do stoichiometric ratios need to be considered in this situation? Explain.

Calculations Involving Limiting Reagents

Textbook pp. 331–335

MAIN IDEA: In any reaction, the limiting reagent will always determine the amount of reactants that react and the amount of product that is produced.

1. If the actual mole ratio of reactant A to reactant B in a reaction is greater than the ideal stoichiometric ratio, then reactant _____ is the excess reagent. K/U

2. If the actual mole ratio of reactant A to reactant B in a reaction is less than the ideal stoichiometric ratio, then reactant _____ is the limiting reagent. K/U

3. The equation $TiCl_4(g) + 2\ Mg(l) \rightarrow Ti(s) + 2\ MgCl_2$ shows how to extract pure titanium, Ti, from titanium tetrachloride, $TiCl_4$. How can you make sure that all of the titanium is extracted from the titanium tetrachloride? K/U

    (a) Use equal masses of titanium tetrachloride and magnesium.

    (b) Use equal molar amounts of titanium tetrachloride and magnesium.

    (c) Use twice as many moles of magnesium as titanium tetrachloride.

    (d) Use more than twice as many moles of magnesium as titanium tetrachloride.

4. The reaction $X + Y \rightarrow Z$ takes place in a closed container. T/I

    (a) If X is the limiting reagent, what would you find in the container after the reaction was complete?

    (b) If X is the excess reagent, what would you find in the container after the reaction was complete?

    (c) If the reaction is carried out to precise stoichiometric values, what would you find in the container after the reaction was complete?

5. Potassium metal tarnishes easily, forming an oxide when it is exposed to oxygen, according to the equation $K(s) + O_2(g) \rightarrow K_2O$. How much tarnish will form in grams when 7.0 moles of K react with 2.4 moles of O_2? T/I

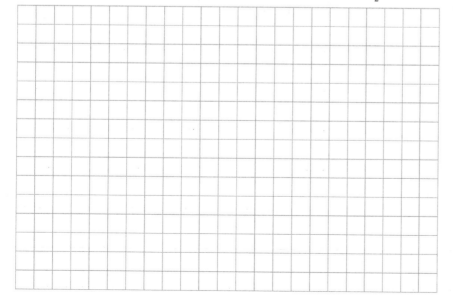

LEARNING **TIP**

6. The reaction $2A + 3B \rightarrow A_2B_3$ takes place in a closed container.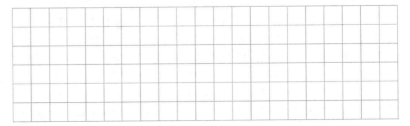

   (a) Five moles of A are placed in the container with 6 moles of B. Which reagent(s) will be left in the container when the reaction is complete?

   (b) How many moles of the product A_2B_3 would be produced from the conditions in part (a)?

7. Potassium metal is extracted from potassium carbonate by heating it with charcoal (carbon): $C(s) + K_2CO_3(s) \rightarrow K(s) + CO_2$. What mass of potassium can be made by combining 20.2 g of carbon and 52.5 g of KCO_3?

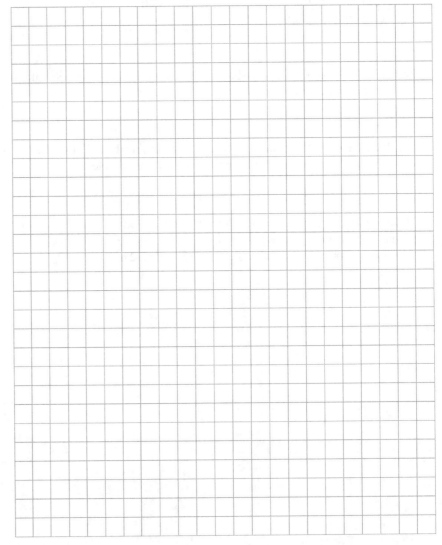

Percentage Yield

Vocabulary

theoretical yield   actual yield   percentage yield

Textbook pp. 336–339

MAIN IDEA: The percentage yield of a reaction can vary depending on a variety of factors, including impurities, poor lab techniques, and reactions that compete with the reaction itself. Percentage yield is defined as

$$\text{percentage yield} = \frac{\text{actual yield}}{\text{theoretical yield}} \times 100\ \%$$

1. The _____ yield of a reaction is usually lower than its _____ yield. K/U

2. Is the following statement true or false? If you think the statement is false, rewrite it to make it true: In winemaking, all of the glucose from the fruit does not get converted to ethanol because the toxicity of the ethanol kills off the organisms that are making it. K/U

> **STUDY TIP**
>
> **Percentage Yield and Mass**
> If you are given the mass of both reactants, you need to identify the limiting reactant before you can go on to calculate the percentage yield.

3. A chemist calculated that a reaction using a reactant that was 75 % pure would theoretically yield 40 g of product. T/I C

   (a) If the reaction yielded 32 g of the product, what was the percentage yield?

   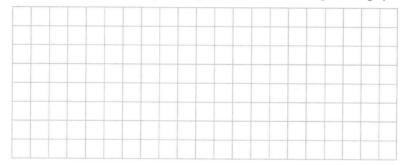

   (b) If the reaction yielded 42 g of the product, what was the percentage yield?

   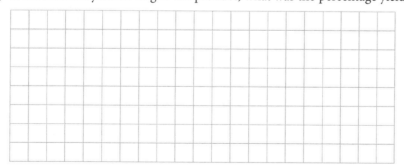

   (c) What might explain the percentage yield in part (b)?

4. Complete **Table 1** to summarize the factors that cause the actual yield of a reaction to be lower than the theoretical yield. K/U C

Table 1 Why Actual Yield Can Be Reduced

Reason for lower actual yield	What happens	Example	Result

5. Aluminum reacts with chlorine according to the equation

$$2 \text{ Al(s)} + 3 \text{ Cl}_2\text{(g)} \rightarrow 2 \text{ AlCl}_3\text{(s)}$$

If 3.8 mol of aluminum reacts with an excess of Cl_2 to produce 1.6 mol of AlCl_3, what is the percentage yield of the reaction? T/I

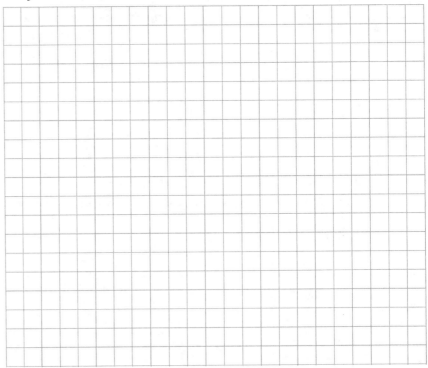

6. Iron (III) oxide forms when iron is heated in the presence of oxygen:

$$Fe(s) + O_2(g) \rightarrow Fe_2O_3(s)$$

If 234.0 g of iron reacts with an excess of oxygen to produce 310.6 g of Fe_2O_3, what is the percentage yield of the reaction? T/I

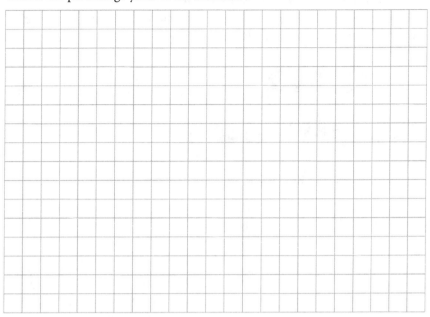

7. A different reaction with iron and oxygen is given by

$$Fe(s) + O_2(g) \rightarrow Fe_3O_4(s)$$

If 380.0 g of iron reacts with 111.1 g of O_2 to produce 302.5 g of Fe_3O_4, what is the percentage yield of the reaction? T/I

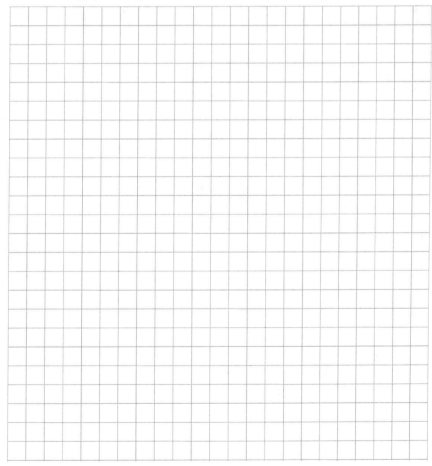

Stoichiometry in Chemical Reactions

Fill in the blanks in the graphic organizer below to summarize the main ideas from Chapter 7. Make additional notes to help you study.

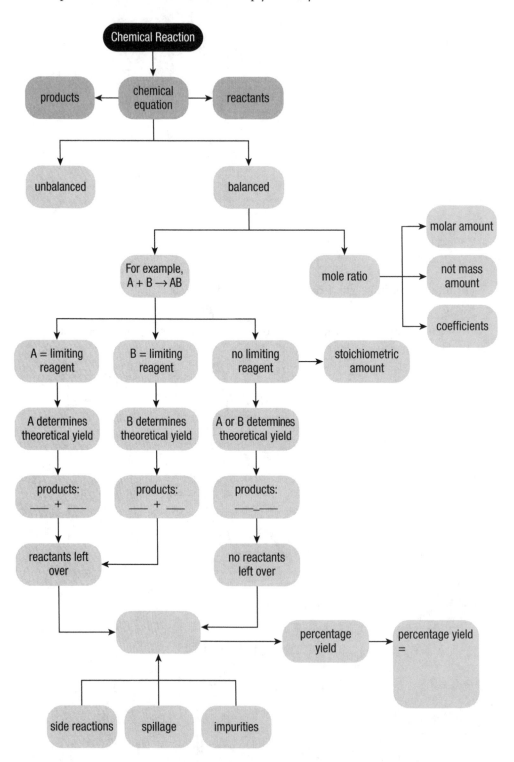

1. Phosphorus burns in oxygen according to the following equation: (7.1) K/U T/I
$$P_4(s) + O_2(g) \rightarrow P_2O_5(g)$$
   (a) Write a balanced equation for the reaction.

   (b) What is the mole ratio between O_2 and P_2O_5 in the equation you wrote for part (a)?

   (c) How many moles of P_4 would you need to produce 1 mole of P_2O_5?

K/U   Knowledge/Understanding
T/I   Thinking/Investigation
C   Communication
A   Application

2. Indicate whether each of the following statements is true or false. If you think the statement is false, rewrite it to make it true. K/U
   (a) If you use stoichiometric amounts in a reaction, you will have only a single reactant left when the reaction is complete. (7.2)

   (b) To save money, companies usually choose to use an excess of the less expensive reagent in a reaction. (7.3)

3. Consider the decomposition reaction of potassium chlorate:
$$2\ KClO_3 \rightarrow 2\ KCl + 3\ O_2$$
   Which of the following shows a stoichiometric amount for each entity? (7.2) T/I
   (a) 245.1 g $KClO_3$, 199.1 g KCl, 96.0 g O_2
   (b) 245.1 g $KClO_3$, 149.1 g KCl, 96.0 g O_2
   (c) 205.1 g $KClO_3$, 199.1 g KCl, 96.0 g O_2
   (d) 205.1 g $KClO_3$, 149.1 g KCl, 144.0 g O_2

4. For the combustion of propane, $C_3H_8(g) + 5\ O_2(g) \rightarrow 3\ CO_2(g) + 4\ H_2O(g)$, 100.0 g of carbon dioxide was produced. How much propane was burned? (7.2) T/I

5. Consider the reaction, $X_2 + Y \rightarrow X_4Y_3$. (7.3) T/I C A
   (a) Write a balanced equation for the reaction.

   (b) Draw a stoichiometric representation of the reaction.

(c) Draw a reaction in which X is the limiting reagent and Y is the excess reagent.

(d) Draw a reaction in which Y is the limiting reagent and X is the excess reagent.

6. Boron reacts with chlorine gas according to this equation:

$$2 B(s) + 3 Cl_2(g) \rightarrow 2 BCl_3(g)$$

A sample of 25.7 g of boron reacts with 200.0 g of Cl_2 to produce 176.4 g of BCl_3. (7.5) T/I A
(a) What is the limiting reagent in this reaction?

(b) What is the theoretical yield of the reaction?

(c) What is the percentage yield of the reaction?

7. For the reaction $A + B \rightarrow C$, how can you calculate the percentage yield of C if you are given m_A, m_B, and m_C? Complete the flow chart (**Figure 1**). (7.5) T/I

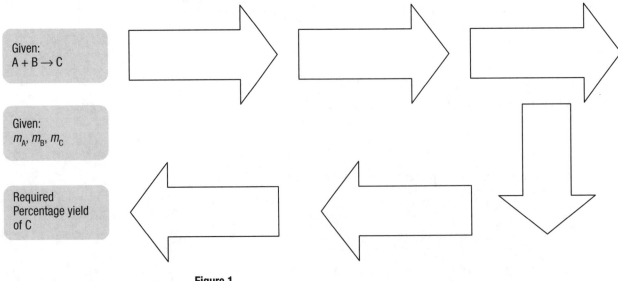

Given:
$A + B \rightarrow C$

Given:
m_A, m_B, m_C

Required
Percentage yield
of C

Figure 1

1. A food company analyzed its new flavour compound and found that it had two different forms—right- and left-handed mirror images of one another. Both compounds have the exact same chemical formula. Yet, company chemists think that there could be a difference in the two compounds. How could you resolve this issue, with a quantitative or a qualitative analysis? (6.1) K/U C A

K/U Knowledge/Understanding
T/I Thinking/Investigation
C Communication
A Application

2. A golf ball has a mass of 45.9 g. A tennis ball has a mass of 56.8 g. Which statement is true for a mole of golf balls and a mole of tennis balls? (6.3, 6.5) K/U T/I A

   (a) The tennis balls would have greater mass, but the quantity of golf balls would be greater.
   (b) Both groups of balls would have the same mass, but there would be fewer tennis balls in number.
   (c) The tennis balls would have greater mass, but the quantity would be the same for both types of ball.
   (d) Both types of ball would be the same in both quantity and mass.

3. Is the following statement true or false? If you think the statement is false, rewrite it to make it true: All compounds with the same empirical formula have the same molar mass. (6.7, 6.9) K/U

4. **Table 1** shows the analysis of compounds A and B, each of which has formula $C_xH_yO_z$. (6.6, 6.7, 6.9) T/I A
   (a) Fill in the missing values in Table 1.

   Table 1 Analysis of Compounds A and B with Formula CxHyOz

Compound	Mass of compound (g)	Mass of carbon (g)	Mass of hydrogen (g)	Mass of oxygen (g)
A	20.0	12.0	1.6	6.4
A	25.0			
B	20.0	8.0	1.3	10.7
B	25.0			

   (b) Write the empirical and molecular formula for each compound shown below.

   empirical formula: _____
   molecular formula: _____

   empirical formula: _____
   molecular formula: _____

   (c) Use your data from part (b) to identify compound A and B from Table 1.

5. Given the equation A + B → C and values for m_A and m_B, complete the flow chart (**Figure 1**) to show how to calculate m_C, the mass of compound C that would result from the reaction (7.3, 7.4) T/I A

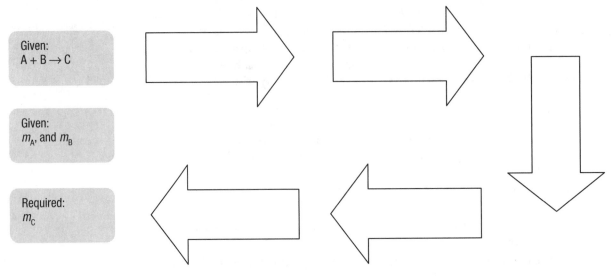

Given:
A + B → C

Given:
m_A, and m_B

Required:
m_C

Figure 1

6. Chromium reacts with fluorine to produce chromium (V) fluoride, CrF_5:

$$2 \, Cr(s) + 5 \, F_2(g) \rightarrow 2 \, CrF_5(s)$$

How many grams of fluorine are required to produce 200.0 g of CrF_5? (7.2) T/I A

7. A chemist combines 250.0 g of copper, Cu, in a container with 48.0 of oxygen, O:

$$4 \, Cu(s) + O_2(g) \rightarrow 2 \, Cu_2O$$

Which reactant will be the limiting reactant in this reaction? the excess reactant? How do you know? (7.3, 7.4) T/I C A

8. Magnesium reacts with nitrogen gas in the reaction

$$3 \, Mg(s) + N_2(g) \rightarrow Mg_3N_2$$

What mass of Mg_3N_2 can be produced by combining 50.0 g of Mg and 30.0 g of N_2 in stoichiometric proportions? (7.4) T/I C A

9. Sulfur reacts with chlorine gas according to the equation

$$S_8(l) + 4 \, Cl_2(g) \rightarrow 4 \, S_2Cl_2(l)$$

to produce sulfur chloride, a compound that has a dreadful smell. A sample of 140.0 g of sulfur reacts with 140.0 g of Cl_2 to produce 58.4 g of S_2Cl_2. (7.5) T/I A

(a) What is the limiting reagent in this the reaction?

(b) What is the theoretical yield of the reaction?

(c) What is the percentage yield of the reaction?

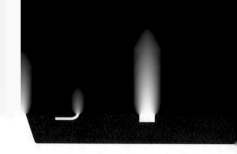

Chapter 8: Water and Solutions

Water is the basis for life and all living organisms. The water cycle powered by the Sun provides Earth's inhabitants with clean water by removing harmful contaminants. Factors such as population growth, an increase in water demand, and pollution are putting a strain on the global water supply.

A solution is a homogeneous mixture of two or more phases (visible parts) that are dissolved in a solvent. The substance present in the lowest quantity is the solute, and the substance present in the highest quantity is the solvent. A saturated solution contains the maximum amount of solute at a given concentration. An unsaturated solution contains less than the maximum solute needed to dissolve. In a supersaturated solution, a solution is forced to dissolve by adding more solute than normal.

Chapter 9: Solutions and Their Reactions

Physical, biological, and chemical water contaminants can cause many adverse effects such as sickness, ecosystem decline, and even death.

Formula equations, total ionic equations, and net ionic equations are used to demonstrate the reaction of ions while in solution. Chemical tests can be used to determine the identity of a substance. Qualitative analysis is the identification of a substance, such as by colour. Stoichiometry can be used to determine the quantity of reactants needed to complete a reaction. Concentration and volume can be used to determine the amount of a given chemical using the amount concentration equation, $n = cv$.

Chapter 10: Acids and Bases

The pH scale is a measure of how acidic or basic a solution is. An acid is classified as a solution that has a pH less than 7, while a base has a pH greater than 7. Acids are named depending on whether they do or do not contain oxygen. Acid base indicators or the systematic naming scheme can be used to identify acids or bases. The Arrhenius theory of acids and bases postulates that when an electrolyte dissolves, its ions dissociate or come apart. This allows them to move freely in the solution and to conduct electricity.

BIG IDEAS

- Properties of solutions can be described qualitatively and quantitatively, and can be predicted.

- Living things depend for their survival on the unique physical and chemical properties of water.

- People have a responsibility to protect the integrity of Earth's water resources.

The Importance of Water

Vocabulary

water cycle   transpiration   aquifer   potable water

MAIN IDEA: Water is essential to the human body. Strong hydrogen bonds are responsible for many of the important physical properties of water.

1. What are three ways in which the human body would be affected if it were suddenly without water? K/U

2. Water has a relatively small molecular mass when compared to similar compounds. Why are forces between water molecules so strong? K/U

3. Fill in **Table 1** to classify each benefit of hydrogen bonds as having physical significance or biological significance. T/I

Table 1 Significance of Hydrogen Bond Benefits

Benefit	Significance
store fats and oils	
make ice float	
maintain body fluids	

4. Describe the hydrogen dipole–dipole forces that are present in water. K/U

5. The water cycle is able to continuously run due to energy from:
   (a) the Sun
   (b) transpiration
   (c) hydrogen bonds
   (d) evaporation K/U

6. The strength of a hydrogen bond increases as the size or _____ of the molecule increases. K/U

7. Draw a diagram to show the hydrogen bond formations present in one molecule of water. C K/U

STUDY TIP

Visualize the Molecule
Water is a polar molecule. The oxygen atom has a slight negative charge and the hydrogen atoms have a slight positive charge. Visualize the molecule, its elements, and each of its charges. This will help you understand how water molecules bond with each other.

MAIN IDEA: The water cycle is crucial to the continuous supply of safe or potable water because the overall amount of water on Earth will not change.

8. Match the terms on the left with the appropriate description on the right. K/U
   (a) surface water
   (b) water table
   (c) groundwater
   (d) potable water

   (i) water that is suitable for human consumption
   (ii) water found in lakes, streams, and rivers that is a primary source of drinking water
   (iii) water that reaches the soil and soaks directly into the ground
   (iv) the upper limit of where ground water permeates the ground

9. As much as 90 % of the water that enters Earth's atmosphere comes from evaporated surface water. Where does the rest of the water in the atmosphere come from? Explain. K/U

10. Create a concept map to describe the three natural water purification processes. K/U C

11. (a) Define "aquifer" in your own words.

    (b) Would you expect a large populated city or a small rural area to use aquifers? Explain. K/U T/I C

12. (a) Why is potable water so important to humans?

(b) What risks are associated with consuming unpurified water? Explain. K/U

13. Consider the water cycle and the rate at which water is replenished in the various parts of the cycle. In which part of the cycle does it take the longest time for water to be replenished? the shortest? K/U

14. What process leaves behind dissolved substances that make ocean water salty? K/U

(a) evaporation
(b) filtration
(c) bacterial action
(d) dissolution

15. Use the subjects of population growth, surface water pollution, and an increasing global demand for water to create a flow chart describing how each contributed to the global water crisis. K/U C

STUDY **TIP**

Follow the Flow
When organizing material for review, consider a flow chart. Flow charts can provide a means to organize material and to understand how concepts are connected. Create a flow chart for the water cycle to show how each of the steps in the process relate to one another.

Solutions and Their Characteristics

Vocabulary

heterogeneous mixture	concentrated solution	alloy	aqueous solution
concentration	dilute solution	amalgam	

Textbook pp. 376–381

MAIN IDEA: Solutions are homogeneous mixtures that are composed of two or more substances, which are uniform throughout the mixture and present in one phase. Heterogeneous mixtures are solutions that consist of two or more visible phases.

1. A mixture seems to have a uniform appearance. What type of mixture would you say it is? K/U
   - (a) homogeneous mixture
   - (b) simple mixture
   - (c) aqueous solution
   - (d) water solution

2. If you have an unknown solution, how can you determine just by looking at it whether it is a homogeneous or heterogeneous mixture? K/U

> **STUDY TIP**
>
> **Take A Look**
> You can often tell whether a solution is homogeneous or heterogeneous by looking for one or two distinctive phases. However, remember that phases may be difficult to distinguish with the unaided eye.

3. Classify each compound in **Table 1** as a heterogeneous mixture or a homogeneous mixture. T/I

Table 1 Types of Mixtures

Compound	Type of Mixture
concrete	
sugar water	
sand in water	
vinegar	

MAIN IDEA: A solution is composed of a solute and a solvent and can be present in different states.

4. The _____ is the component of the solution that is present in the greatest quantity. K/U

5. Indicate whether each statement is true or false. If you think the statement is false, rewrite it to make it true. K/U

   (a) The most important characteristic of solutions is that their state of matter stays the same.

   (b) Solutions can be solids, liquids, or gases.

6. Determine the solute and solvent for each solution in **Table 2**. T/I

Table 2 Solutes and Solvents

Solution	Solute	Solvent
salt water		
carbonated beverage (carbon dioxide and water)		
sugar water		
rubbing alcohol (60 % isopropyl alcohol)		

7. _____ is the relationship between the quantity of solute versus the overall quantity of solution or solvent. K/U

8. Can metals form solutions? Explain. K/U

The Dissolving Process

Vocabulary				Textbook pp. 382–389
hydration	miscible	immiscible	surfactant	
dissociation				

MAIN IDEA: The solubility of a substance in water or another solvent is dependent on its molecular makeup.

1. In a dissociation equation, what is written on the left side of the equation? K/U
   (a) ions
   (b) solid compound
   (c) water
   (d) alloy

2. Write a chemical equation for the dissociation of sodium hydroxide, NaOH(s). C

> **STUDY TIP**
>
> **Consider Your Experiences**
> Most of us have had experiences with solubility. Have you ever dissolved sugar into water? Keep these experiences in mind when thinking about solubility and the way in which compounds dissolve in solution.

3. Indicate whether each statement is true or false. If you think the statement is false, rewrite it to make it true. K/U
   (a) During dissociation, ions combine and form one compound.

   (b) Liquids that completely mix with each other when they come in contact are immiscible.

4. Briefly explain why some compounds easily mix with water while others do not. T/I

MAIN IDEA: Solutes generally readily dissolve in solvents that possess a similar polarity. Water, a polar compound, does not mix with non-polar hydrocarbons.

5. Explain why hydrocarbons are immiscible in water.

6. Fill in **Table 1** to describe the dissolving behaviour of solutes and solvents when they combine. T/I A

Table 1 Behaviour of Solutes and Solvents

Compound or Solute	Solvent	Dissolve (yes or no)
ionic compound	polar solvent	
non-polar solute		no
	non-polar solvent	yes

MAIN IDEA: Surfactants are compounds that reduce the surface tension of a solvent. They can be used to introduce the mix of polar and non-polar solvents.

7. Two of the most well known surfactants are _____ and _____. K/U

8. Soaps are made by reacting animal _____ or vegetable _____ with a concentrated _____. K/U

9. What role do surfactants play in oil spills? K/U

Oil Dispersants—Is the Fix Worse than the Problem?

Textbook pp. 390–391

MAIN IDEA: Environmental hazards posed by oil rigs can be mitigated through the use of dispersants. Dispersants can have a negative impact on the environment as well.

1. Taking into account what you have learned about oil and water thus far, what characteristics of oil make it a little easier to treat during an oil spill? K/U T/I

2. Fill in **Table 1** to show two benefits and two risks of offshore oil drilling. K/U C

Table 1 Benefits and Risks of Offshore Oil Drilling

Benefits	Risks

3. How do dispersants work to clean up oil spills? K/U

4. Describe at least three things that can be done to better prepare for potential oil spills in the future. A

Solubility and Saturation

Vocabulary

saturated solution   supersaturated solution   thermal pollution   pressure

unsaturated solution   solubility curve

MAIN IDEA: At a given temperature, a solution can be saturated, unsaturated, or supersaturated. A solubility curve can be used to demonstrate the relationship between the solubility of a solute and temperature.

1. If you add more solute to a solution and the solute dissolves, what type of solution do you have? K/U
   (a) supersaturated solution
   (b) saturated solution
   (c) unsaturated solution
   (d) concentrated solution

2. A _____ solution is a solution that has been forced to dissolve more solute. K/U

3. Is the following statement true or false? If you think the statement is false, rewrite it to make it true: Supersaturated solutions are stable. K/U

> **LEARNING TIP**
>
> **Concentration and Solubility**
> Concentration and solubility are similar concepts. Concentration describes the quantity of solute per unit volume of solution. Solubility, however, describes the maximum quantity of solute that will dissolve per unit volume at a given temperature. The concentration of glucose (sugar) in a sports drink, for example, may be 6.2 g/mL. But the solubility of glucose in water is 91 g/100 mL at 25 °C. That means that much more glucose could potentially dissolve in a sports drink.

4. Examine the solubility curve of salt in 100 g of water in **Figure 1**. T/I

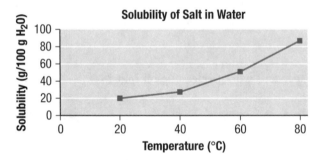

Figure 1

(a) What mass of salt would dissolve in 100 g of water at 20 °C?
   _____

(b) What can you conclude about the solubility of the solutions based on the four data points?

(c) If you add 10 g of salt to 100 g of water at about 30 °C, it would be a(n) _____ solution.

> **LEARNING TIP**
>
> **Interpreting Solubility Curves**
> Three labels define the different parts of the graph.
>
> supersaturated
> saturated
> unsaturated
> Solubility / Temperature

MAIN IDEA: Pressure can affect the solubility of a gas.

5. Define pressure in your own words. K/U C

6. How can you use a solubility curve to determine how many additional grams of solute are needed to make a saturated solution? K/U

7. _____ water contains more dissolved oxygen than _____ water. K/U

8. Why does bottled pop become flat after a few days, even though you have tightly screwed the cap back on? A

> **STUDY TIP**
>
> **Understanding Solubility Graphs**
> To create a solubility graph, you need to measure the solubility of a substance at a given temperature. This is done by calculating the mass of the solute needed to make a saturated solution. This measurement is repeated for temperatures from 0 °C to 100 °C with each of the points plotted on a solubility graph. A line is then drawn to connect the points.

9. What factors affect the solubilty in solids and gases? Describe the relationship. K/U

10. Describe the effect that pressure has on the solubility of solids, liquids, and gases. Explain why. K/U T/I

11. An environmentalist notices that the aquatic wildlife in a lake located near a power plant in the area has twice the mortality rate when compared to similar areas farther away from the power plant. Give a reasonable explanation for this. A

12. Why do unrefrigerated beverages fizz when you pour them onto ice? K/U A

Concentration

> **Vocabulary**
>
> amount concentration (c)   stock solution   standard solution

MAIN IDEA: Concentrated solutions contain a large amount of dissolved solute per unit volume of solution.

1. A concentrated solution that will be diluted prior to use is a:
   (a) concentrated solution
   (b) stock solution
   (c) dilute solution
   (d) saturated solution K/U

2. While working with hydrochloric acid and water, your lab partner's beaker suddenly shatters. Why might this have occurred? T/I

3. What is the difference between a concentrated solution and a dilute solution? K/U

4. You know the concentration and the volume of a solution. How can you determine the amount of solute? K/U

5. When using the amount concentration formula, what three things should you check for before you begin? K/U
   (i)

   (ii)

   (iii)

MAIN IDEA: Solutions are prepared using known concentrations or standard solutions. The amount of concentration can be determined by using the equation $c = n/V$, where c is the amount of concentration, n is the amount of solute in mol, and V is the volume of the solution in L.

6. What is the name for a solution of known concentration? K/U
   (a) saturated solution
   (b) standard solution
   (c) concentrated solution
   (d) stock solution

7. A 50 L sample of concentrated sodium hydroxide, NaOH, contains 40 g of sodium, Na. Calculate the amount concentration of the solution. T/I

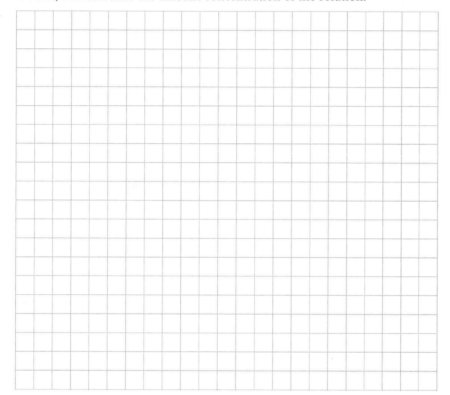

Preparing Dilutions

Textbook pp. 403–405

> **Vocabulary**
>
> dilution

MAIN IDEA: Solutes are diluted in order to decrease the concentration. For analytical dilutions, especially those that require small volumes, volumetric glassware is used to ensure better precision.

1. What would you need to add to sodium hydroxide in order to dilute it? K/U
   (a) sodium hydroxide
   (b) water
   (c) both a and b
   (d) none of the above

2. For each type of volumetric glassware listed in **Table 1**, describe when you would use it, and comment on its precision. K/U

   Table 1 Types of Volumetric Glassware

Volumetric Glassware	When you might use it	Precision
volumetric pipette		
graduated pipette		
graduated cylinder		
volumetric flask		

STUDY TIP

Volumetric Dilutions
Precision is very important when doing dilutions. Make sure each measurement is precise to ensure that your solution is the right concentration. For certain experiments, if the concentration is not just right, you will not get the desired results.

3. Is the following statement true or false? If you think the statement is false, rewrite it to make it true: During a dilution, the total amount of moles in the solution increases due to an increase in volume. K/U

4. A scientist performs a dilution of a 10 mol/L acid solution. Has the concentration of the solution changed? K/U T/I

5. During a dilution, the amount of moles in the solute _____ . K/U
   (a) decreases
   (b) increases
   (c) stays the same
   (d) expands

MAIN IDEA: The dilution equation can be used in the lab to solve dilution problems. This is represented mathematically as $c_c V_c = c_d V_d$.

6. What volume of 10.0 mol/L hydrochloric acid, HCl, is needed to make 400 mL of 0.250 mol/L HCl solution? T/I

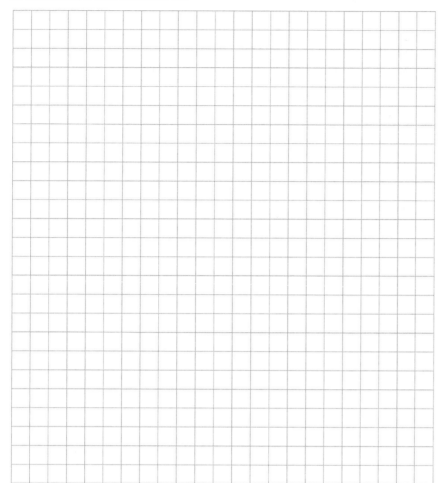

Dilution Equation

$c_c V_c = c_d V_d$

c_c is the concentration of the concentrated solution

V_c is the volume of the concentrated solution

c_d is the concentration of the dilute solution

V_d is the volume of the dilute solution

LEARNING **TIP**

Dilution Factors

A quick way to determine the final concentration of a dilute solution is by multiplying c_c by a dilution factor. The dilution factor is the volume of the concentrated solution divided by the volume of the dilute solution. In Sample Problem 1 on p. 404 of the Student Book, the dilution factor is 0.250/4.5 (see Step 2). Chemists routinely use dilution factors when preparing solutions.

Concentrations and Consumer Products

LEARNING **TIP**

Weight and Mass
In everyday language, "weight" and "mass" are often used interchangeably. Remember, however, that they are not the same. Used correctly, "mass" is the quantity of substance and is measured in grams or kilograms. "Weight" is the force of gravity on the object and is measured in newtons. You would weigh much less on the Moon than on Earth, because gravity is not so strong there. Of course, your mass would be unchanged.

MAIN IDEA: The concentration of consumer products, as well as lab and environmental compounds, can be displayed using several different units. **Table 1** summarizes some of the ways concentration is expressed.

Table 1 Measure of Concentration

Name	Abbreviation	Equation	Application
percentage volume/volume	% V/V	$C_{v/v} = \dfrac{V_{solute}}{V_{solution}} \times 100\,\%$	liquid–liquid mixtures
percentage weight/volume	% W/V	$C_{w/v} = \dfrac{m_{solute}}{V_{solution}} \times 100\,\%$	solid–liquid mixtures
percentage weight/weight	% W/W	$C_{w/w} = \dfrac{m_{solute}}{m_{solution}} \times 100\,\%$	solid–liquid or solid–solid mixtures
parts per million	ppm	$C_{ppm} = \dfrac{m_{solute}}{m_{solution}} \times 10^6\,\text{ppm}$	to express small concentrations (e.g., composition of air)
parts per billion	ppb	$C_{ppb} = \dfrac{m_{solute}}{m_{solution}} \times 10^9\,\text{ppb}$	to express very small concentrations (e.g., metal contaminants in water)
parts per trillion	ppt	$C_{ppt} = \dfrac{m_{solute}}{m_{solution}} \times 10^{12}\,\text{ppt}$	to express extremely small concentrations (e.g., traces of medications in water

1. Provide another equation that can be used to calculate concentration. **K/U**

LEARNING **TIP**

Working with Percentages
1. Remember that a percentage is a fraction of 100. In fact, you can think of the percent symbol (%) as containing a "1" and two zeros.
2. To determine the percentage of a number, remember that the word "of" means "multiplied by." Simply multiply the number by the percentage written as a decimal. For example,
13.5 % of 750 = (0.135)(750) = 101

2. The label on a bottle of drain cleaner indicates that it is 30 % sulfuric acid by volume. What is the percentage volume/volume of the solution (% V/V)? **T/I** **C**

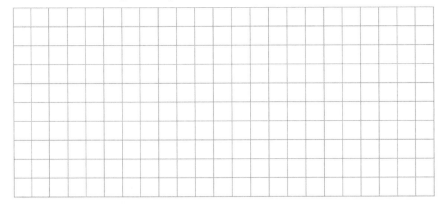

3. What is the density of water at 20 °C? **K/U**

4. What is the density of very dilute aqueous solutions? Why? K/U

5. Which one of the following is the same as saying 10 ppm of glucose? K/U
   (a) 10 parts of glucose for every million parts of solution
   (b) 10 parts of glucose for every billion parts of solution
   (c) 10 % of glucose for every 10 % of solution
   (d) 10 L of glucose for every 10 % of solution

6. What volume of a 2.0 % W/V glucose solution can be made with 200 g of glucose? T/I

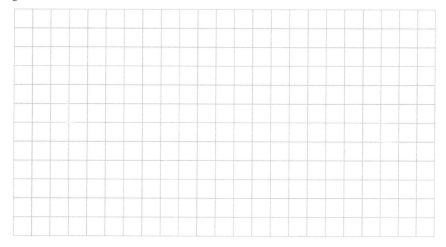

LEARNING TIP

Percentages and Exponents
"ppm" is similar to the symbol "%" in the equations involving percentage concentration. You could think of the "× 100" in the equations from Table 1 as "× 10^2." You could even think of "%" as "pph"—parts per hundred!

7. _____ is the force of gravity exerted on an object. K/U

8. A package of cortisone cream has a percentage weight/weight of 2 % hydrocortisone. What does the % W/W tell you? K/U

9. 0.300 L of 45 % sodium hydroxide is diluted to 4.000 L. Determine the final concentration of the solution. T/I

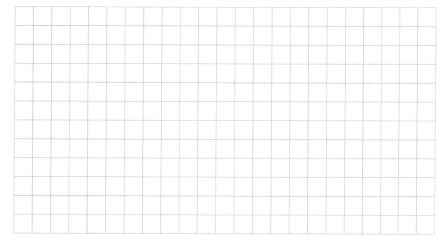

STUDY TIP

Organize the Information
Percentage concentration can be measured by percentage volume/volume, percentage weight/volume, and percentage weight/weight. To organize these measurements, create a chart or table that allows you to identify how to calculate each measure.

10. How do scientists generally express very dilute concentrations? K/U

Water and Solutions

The graphic organizer below summarizes some of the main ideas from Chapter 8. Fill in the missing information and add your own notes to help you study.

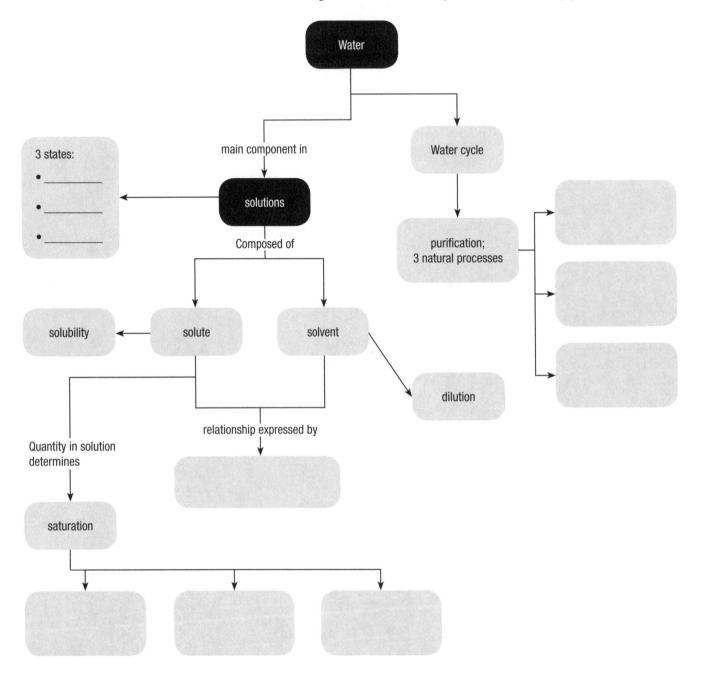

1. Which property of water allows life to exist below sheets of ice in the Arctic? (8.1) K/U
   (a) high surface tension
   (b) expansion when cooling from 4 °C to 0 °C
   (c) high melting and boiling points
   (d) ability to exchange thermal energy with little change in temperature

2. Is each of the following statements true or false? If you think the statement is false, rewrite it to make it true. K/U
   (a) Intermolecular forces decrease as the size or polarity of the molecule increases. (8.1)

   (b) A solution that contains a high quantity of solute compared to the total volume of solution is a dilute solution. (8.2)

   (c) Dissociation is the process that occurs when ions are surrounded by water molecules. (8.3)

3. Explain why air can be classified as a homogeneous and heterogeneous mixture. (8.2) K/U T/I

4. List three properties of water that are the result of hydrogen bonding. (8.1) K/U

5. What is an aqueous solution? (8.2) K/U

6. Fill in **Table 1** to compare and contrast the effect that increasing temperature and pressure have on the solubility of solids, liquids, and gases. (8.5) K/U T/I

Table 1 Factors Affecting Solubility of Liquids, Gases, and Solids

Factor	Liquids	Gases	Solids
increase in temperature			
increase in pressure			

7. Consider the following solubility curve for glucose in water (**Figure 1**). T/I C

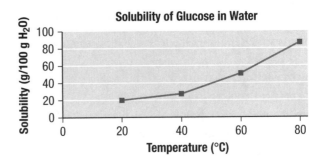

Solubility of Glucose in Water

Figure 1

(a) At 20 °C, what is the maximum amount of glucose that will dissolve in water?

(b) Looking at the graph, what can you conclude about the relationship between solubility and temperature for glucose?

(c) What is the level of saturation of 60 g glucose/100 g H_2O at 40 °C?

(d) How much additional glucose in grams would be required to saturate 5 g of glucose at 20 °C?

8. Complete the graphic organizer below (**Figure 2**), identifying and describing the three degrees of saturation for a solution. (8.5) K/U

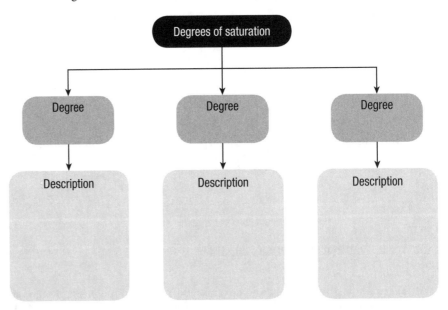

Figure 2

Reactions of Ions in Solution

Textbook pp. 424–428

Vocabulary

formula equation   total ionic equation   spectator ions   net ionic equations

MAIN IDEA: Reactions between ions in solution can be demonstrated using formula equations. A solubility table (**Table 1**) can be used to determine which compounds actually precipitate and which compounds remain dissolved.

Table 1 Solubility of Ionic Compounds at Room Temperature

Solubility	Ion	Exceptions
very soluble (aq) ≥ 0.1 mol/L	NO_3^-	none
	Cl^- and other halides	except with Cu^+, Ag^+, Hg_2^{2+}, Pb^{2+}
	SO_4^{2-}	except with Ca^{2+}, Ba^{2+}, Sr^{2+}, Hg^{2+}, Pb^{2+}, Ag^+
	$C_2H_3O_2^-$	Ag^+
	Na^+ and K^+	none
	NH_4^+	none
slightly soluble (s) < 0.1 mol/L	CO_3^{2-}	except with Group 1 ions and NH_4^+
	PO_4^{3-}	except with Group 1 ions and NH_4^+
	OH^-	except with Group 1 ions, Ca^{2+}, Ba^{2+}, Sr^{2+}
	S^{2-}	except with Group 1 and 2 ions and NH_4^+

STUDY **TIP**

Solubility Table
Solubility is an important tool in understanding the behaviour of chemical reactions. Although there may be substances that fall outside the general guidelines, by understanding the solubility table, you can use it to write almost any chemical reaction.

1. List the three ways that the reaction of ions in solutions can be represented.
   (i)
   (ii)
   (iii)

2. Complete the concept map (**Figure 1**) below, providing a description of the three ways that the reactions of ions in solution can be represented

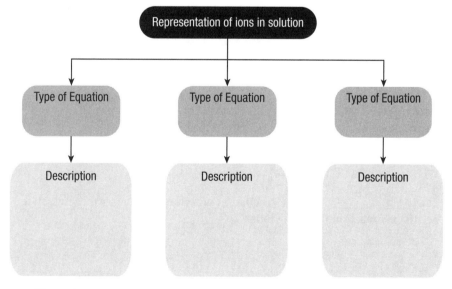

Figure 1

3. For **Table 2**, determine whether the compounds are very soluble (aq) or slightly soluble (s). K/U

Table 2 Solubility of Compounds

Compound	Solubility (aq) or (s)
NaCl	
Ag_2SO_4	
NaOH	
$(NH_4)_2S$	

4. Ions that do not participate in a reaction are known as _____. K/U
   (a) spectator ions
   (b) charged particles
   (c) thermal particles
   (d) precipitants

5. When is a chemical equation considered balanced? K/U

STUDY TIP

Keep Your Balance

Make sure your chemical equation is balanced. The number of ions as well as the electrical charge must agree on both sides of the equation in order for the reaction to be correctly displayed. This is especially important when doing an experiment.

6. Is the following statement true or false? If you think the statement is false, rewrite it to make it true: Ions that do not participate in the reaction are called extra ions. K/U

7. Write a total ionic equation to show the reaction of $CaCl_2$ with K_3PO_4. T/I C

8. Would a reaction occur between barium nitrate, $Ba(NO_3)_2$, and water? How do you know? T/I

9. How are ions that appear on both sides of a total ionic equation affected during a chemical reaction? K/U

10. The _____ equation describes the chemical change that occurs in a reaction involving ions. K/U

11. Use **Table 1** above to answer the following questions.

    (a) Write the total ionic equation and net ionic equation for the reaction between barium sulfate, $BaSO_4$, and potassium sulfide, K_2S.

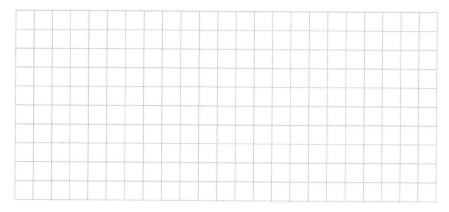

    (b) Which ions are considered spectator ions?

Water Treatment

Textbook pp. 429–436

Vocabulary		
leachate	hard water	soft water

MAIN IDEA: Physical, biological, and chemical substances are responsible for water contamination, so it is important that water quality standards and guidelines be set and followed closely to ensure safe drinking water.

1. What is one of the most important initial steps for improving water quality? Explain. Provide examples. K/U

2. For each type of water contaminant listed in **Table 1**, provide an example and indicate its source.

Table 1 Types of Water Contaminants

Contaminant	Example	Source
physical		
biological		
chemical		

3. _____ is fluid that has passed through solid waste material and has extracted suspended or dissolved substances from mines or dump sites. K/U

4. Is the following statement true or false? If you think the statement is false, rewrite it to make it true: Physical, biological, and chemical contaminants form heterogeneous mixtures with water. K/U

MAIN IDEA: Water treatment processes are extremely important to the production of safe drinking water.

Table 2 Maximum Acceptable Concentrations of Selected Chemicals in Drinking Water

Substance	Typical source	MAC (ppm)
arsenic	mining waste	0.010
cyanide	mining waste	0.2
nitrate	agricultural runoff	45
cadmium	leachate from landfill	0.005

5. If you live near a coal mine, according to **Table 2** above, what substances are most likely to contaminate your water supply? [A]

6. What type of water contains a high concentration of Ca^{2+}, Mg^{2+}, and Fe^{3+} ions? [K/U]
   (a) soft water
   (b) contaminated water
   (c) hard water
   (d) lake water

7. Why can hard water be problematic for residents? [K/U] [T/I]

8. Draw a flow chart to show what happens during softening, aeration, and disinfection in a typical water treatment process. [K/U] [C]

STUDY TIP

Measuring Water Contamination
Water contaminants are measured in parts per million or ppm. If a pollutant such as arsenic has a concentration of 10 ppm, this means that there are 10 parts of the pollutant in 1 million parts of water.

Chemical Analysis

Textbook pp. 437–441

Vocabulary	
filtrate	flame test

MAIN IDEA: Qualitative chemical analysis can help identify a substance. Quantitative chemical analysis can be used to determine how much of a particular substance is present.

1. What two criteria are generally used to identify a substance? K/U

2. In **Table 1**, indicate whether the testing methods are quantitative, qualitative, or both. K/U

Table 1 Chemical Analysis Test

Test method	Chemical analysis
pH	
hormone concentration in blood sample	
nickel test paper	
breathalyzer	

3. When doing a qualitative analysis test, how do you ensure that the ions present are identified? K/U T/I

4. The _____ is the clear liquid that remains after a mixture has been filtered. K/U

5. Using the solubility table (**Table 1**) from Section 9.1, construct a flow chart that shows the qualitative analysis of a solution that may contain copper(I) ions, $Cu^+(aq)$, and/or zinc ions, $Zn^{2+}(aq)$. C

6. Is the following statement true or false? If you think the statement is false, rewrite it to make it true: Spectroscopy is not helpful in quantitative and qualitative analysis. K/U

Chemistry JOURNAL

Drugs in Drinking Water

Textbook pp. 442–443

MAIN IDEA: A large number of prescription medications are present in the water supply. The low concentrations present have not yet shown any adverse health effects. However, future water treatment technologies may be able to remove the medication.

1. Fill in the fishbone diagram (**Figure 1**) to summarize the main ideas about drugs in drinking water. K/U C

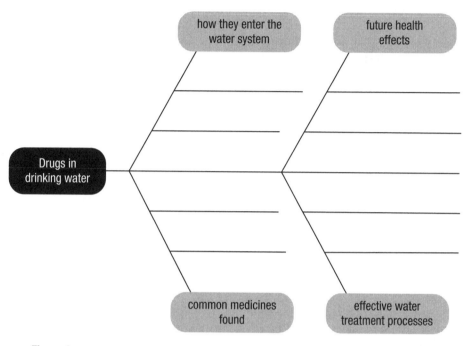

Figure 1

2. Based on what you have read, is it a good idea to flush your medications down the toilet? Explain. K/U A

3. Based on what you have learned up to this point, what other types of substances cannot be dissolved by the body? K/U T/I

Stoichiometry of Solutions

Textbook pp. 444–449

MAIN IDEA: In order for a chemical process to be successful, it is often necessary to know the quantity of the products or reactions. Stoichiometry can be used to predict the quantity of chemicals required for a chemical reaction to occur. The equation $n = c \times v$ can be used to determine the concentration of a substance.

1. Why do chemists often use aqueous solutions to conduct their experiments? **K/U**

2. Based on what you have learned up to now, what is used to determine the ratio of chemicals involved in the final solution? **K/U**
   (a) balanced chemical equation
   (b) solubility
   (c) net equation
   (d) skeleton equation

3. What is one advantage of allowing reactions to occur in solution? **K/U** **T/I**

4. List the three strategies used to solve stoichiometry problems. **K/U**

5. Is the following statement true or false? If you think the statement is false, rewrite it to make it true: Chemicals mix more completely when they are dissolved, resulting in slower reactions. **K/U**

6. Determine the minimum volume of 0.25 mol/L silver nitrate, $AgNO_3$, required to react completely with the sodium ions in 0.250 L of a 0.05 mol/L sodium chloride, NaCl, solution. **T/I**

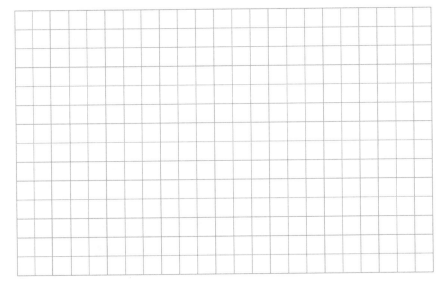

7. Write the dissociation equation for $BaCl_2$. [C]

STUDY TIP

Solutions
The dissociation equation can help to predict the behaviour of ions when in solution. The information can then be used to find the exact concentration of ions present.

8. Why do researchers consider calcium chloride a good electrolyte? [T/I]

9. What type of equation has to be written in order to calculate the amount concentration of each ion that is released when a compound dissolves? [K/U]
   (a) formula equation
   (b) balanced equation
   (c) dissociation equation
   (d) net ionic equation

10. Your lab experiment requires 30.5 g of lead phosphate, $Pb_3(PO_4)_2$, to prepare 525 mL of solution. What are the amount concentrations of lead ions and phosphate ions in the solution? Molecular weight $Pb_3(PO_4)_2 = 811.54$ [T/I]

LEARNING TIP

Ion Concentrations
The concentration of the ions is not always the same as the concentration of the compound they came from. In this case, when $CaCl_2$ dissociates, the chloride concentration will always be double the calcium chloride concentration since 9 chloride ions are released per formula unit of $CaCl_2$.

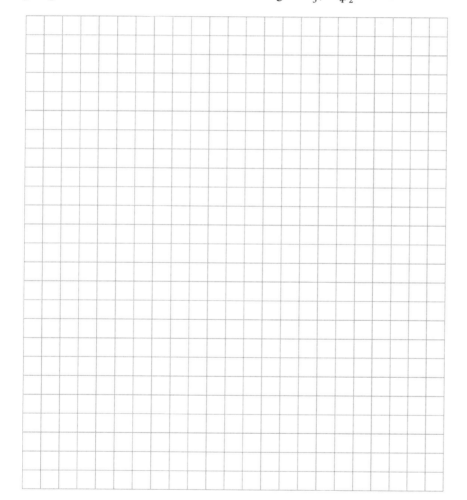

Solutions and Their Reactions

Water is one of the most important aqueous solutions and is used widely in chemical reactions. Using solubility information, chemical reaction equations can be created to demonstrate the behaviour of ions when placed in solution. Chemical analysis tests can also be conducted to determine the ions present.

The graphic organizer below summarizes some of the main ideas from Chapter 9. Add notes as you work through this chapter to help you study.

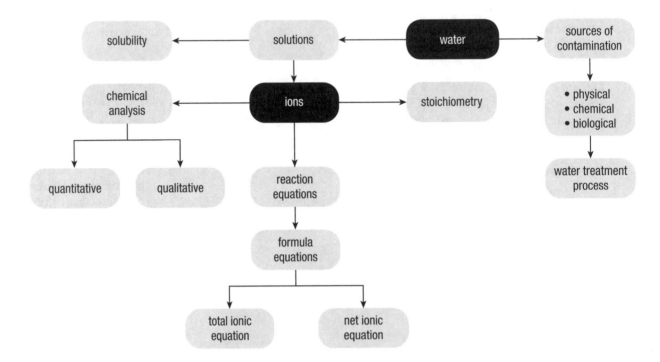

1. _____ is the chemical analysis that describes the concentration of a substance. 9.3 K/U
   (a) quantitative analysis
   (b) qualitative analysis
   (c) ionic equation
   (d) solubility

2. Is the following statement true or false? If the statement is false, rewrite it so that it is true: Chemical contaminants form heterogeneous mixtures with water. (9.2) K/U

3. In a _____ equation, all of the compounds are represented by their chemical formulas. (9.1) K/U

4. Is the following equation balanced? If not, rewrite it so that it is balanced. (9.1) C
$$Pb(OH)_2 + HCl \longrightarrow PbCl_2 + H_2O$$

5. Refer to the solubility table (**Table 1**) from Section 9.1 to answer the following questions. (9.1) K/U T/I C
   (a) Write the total ionic equation and net ionic equation for the reaction of calcium carbonate, $CaCO_3$, and barium chloride, $BaCl_2$.

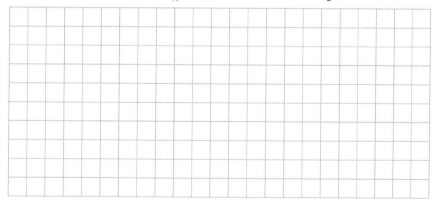

   (b) Name the spectator ions in part (a).

6. Describe how some metal ions can be identified in solutions. (9.3) T/I

7. Fill in the chart in **Table 1** to show the three types of contaminants that are found in water and their possible sources as well as any health or possible environmental impacts. (9.2) K/U

Table 1 Types of Contaminants

Contaminants	Source	Effect
physical		
biological		
chemical		

8. Write the dissociation equation for the reaction between potassium and chloride. (9.5) C

Properties of Acids and Bases

Vocabulary	
oxyacid	

Textbook pp. 464–469

MAIN IDEA: Many of the products that we use and consume contain acids or bases.

1. Name two ways that we consume acidic foods in our daily diet. K/U

2. What type of ions in acidic fluids break down tooth enamel? K/U
   - (a) metal
   - (b) hydrogen
   - (c) calcium
   - (d) aluminum

3. The process of _____ causes teeth to soften. K/U

MAIN IDEA: Acids and bases both have certain characteristics, such as reactivity, that distinguish them from each other.

4. Name two characteristic properties of acids. K/U

5. Name two characteristic properties of bases. K/U

6. When acids and metals react, _____ and _____ are produced. K/U

7. Is the following statement true or false? If you think the statement is false, rewrite it to make it true: When a base reacts with carbon dioxide, oxygen is formed. K/U

> **LEARNING TIP**
>
> **"Alkali" in the Periodic Table**
> The elements in Group 1 are sometimes called "alkali metals." Recall that the oxides of these metals form basic solutions. Similarly, Group 2 elements are the alkaline earth metals. They, too, react to form basic solutions. Basic = alkali.

8. In a chemical equation, how can you usually tell if a compound is an acid? K/U

9. For **Table 1**, determine whether each property described relates to an acid or a base. K/U

Table 1 Acid and Base Properties

Property	Acid or base
pH of 9	
sour taste	
no special feel	

MAIN IDEA: Chemists have developed a systematic method of naming acids and bases.

10. **Table 2** lists the oxyanions that contain the same elements as the chlorate ion, ClO_3^-. K/U

Table 2

Anion	Formula
perchlorate	ClO_4^-
chlorate	ClO_3^-
chlorite	ClO_2^-
hypochlorite	ClO^-

(a) Write the name of the acid with formula $HClO_2(aq)$.

(b) What is the oxyanion?

11. When do hydroxide bases show their basic properties? K/U

Theoretical Acid–Base Definitions

Vocabulary

ionization   strong acid   weak acid

Textbook pp. 470–475

MAIN IDEA: Arrhenius's theory states that acids ionize in water to produce hydrogen ions, and bases dissociate in water and produce hydroxide ions.

1. Make notes about Arrhenius's theory in the main idea web below (**Figure 1**).

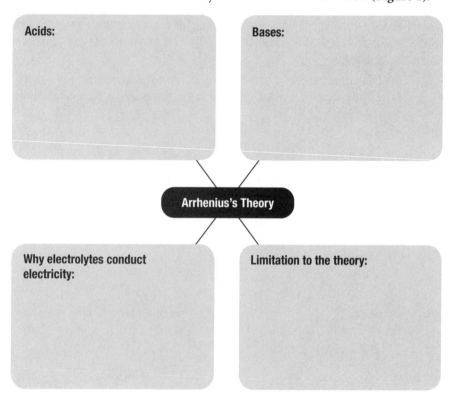

Acids:

Bases:

Arrhenius's Theory

Why electrolytes conduct electricity:

Limitation to the theory:

Figure 1

LEARNING TIP

Dissociation and Ionization
Both dissociation and ionization result in the presence of ions in solution. Dissociation separates ions that already exist in the neutral compound.

$$M^+X^- (s) \rightarrow M^+(aq) + X^-(aq)$$

During ionization, new ions form from a neutral compound.

$$HA(aq) \rightarrow H^+(aq) + A^-(aq)$$

---

2. During the process of _____ , individual ions separate from an ionic compound as it dissolves in water. K/U

3. Write the chemical formula that can be used to simplify an acid–base neutralization reaction. K/U

4. _____ involves the formation of ions from uncharged molecules. K/U

5. Show the complete neutralization reaction from beginning to end for the reaction of potassium hydroxide, KOH(s), and nitric acid, HNO_3(aq). **C**

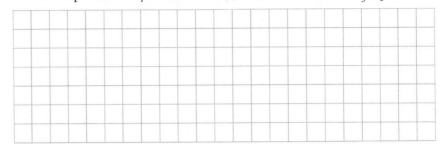

MAIN IDEA: Acids can be classified as strong or weak, and this affects the extent to which they ionize as well as conduct electricity. The pH scale is used to compare how acidic or basic a solution is.

6. Is the following statement true or false? If you think the statement is false, rewrite it to make it true: A weak acid is a substance that completely ionizes in water. **K/U**

7. Explain why some acids do not conduct electricity as well as others. **K/U**

8. A change of _____ pH unit represents a tenfold change in how acidic or basic a solution is. **K/U**

Acid–Base Stoichiometry

Vocabulary

titration	burette	end point
titrant	equivalence point	primary standard

Textbook pp. 476–485

MAIN IDEA: Titration is one of the most common ways to determine the concentration of a solution. It is widely used with acids and bases.

1. Is the following statement true or false? If you think the statement is false, rewrite it to make it true: The point during an acid–base titration when neutralization is complete is called the equivalence point. K/U

> **LEARNING TIP**
>
> **Indicator Solvents**
> Some indicators are compounds dissolved in ethanol, which makes them flammable. They should be handled with care and kept away from flames and sparks.

2. When performing an acid–base titration in the lab, how can you determine when you have reached the equivalence point? K/U

3. Is the following statement true or false? If you think the statement is false, rewrite it to make it true: Acid–base indicators change colour at a specific pH value. K/U

> **LEARNING TIP**
>
> **Cleaning Equipment**
> All laboratory equipment should be cleaned before being stored. To clean burettes and pipettes, first drain them, then rinse them with acetic acid (vinegar), and then with distilled water.

4. During a titration, what things should you pay careful attention to? K/U

> **STUDY TIP**
>
> **Not the Same**
> It is easy to confuse equivalence point and endpoint, but it is important to note that they are different. The equivalence point generally cannot be seen with the naked eye. However, the endpoint can occur suddenly and gives a characteristic change such as colour or pH.

5. Explain what is meant by the "endpoint." K/U

MAIN IDEA: Acid–base indicators can give you an approximate pH of unknown solutions from colour changes, as well as determine whether it is an acid or a base.

6. Use **Table 1** to answer the following questions. K/U A

Table 1 Common Acid–Base Indicators

Indicator	Acid colour	Base colour	pH range
methyl red	red	yellow	4.4 to 6.2
thymol blue	red / yellow	yellow/ blue	1.2 to 2.8 / 8.0 to 9.6
phenolphthalein	yellow	red	10.1 to 12.0

(a) You add methyl red to an unknown solution. The solution turns yellow. Is the solution an acid or a base?

(b) Which indicator(s) could you use to determine whether a substance is a base?

STUDY TIP

Accurate Titrations
When titrating, pay attention as you add each drop. The colour can change suddenly, and you want to make sure that you have an accurate volume amount.

7. A titration gives accurate results only when _____ _____. K/U

8. A titration is performed using 250 mL of an acid. After the titration is completed, the volume of the solution is about 275 mL. What volume of titrant was used in the experiment? T/I

9. A chemical that is highly pure and chemically stable is a _____. K/U

MAIN IDEA: Concentration can also be determined using the amount of concentration equation.

10. A 0.425 g mass of potassium carbonate, K_2CO_3, is dissolved in 0.150 L of water. The solution is titrated with hydrochloric acid, HCl, of unknown concentration. We know that 0.255 L of hydrochloric acid solution was used to titrate the potassium carbonate sample to the endpoint. Calculate the amount concentration of the HCl. The molar mass of K_2CO_3 is 138.21 g/mol. T/I

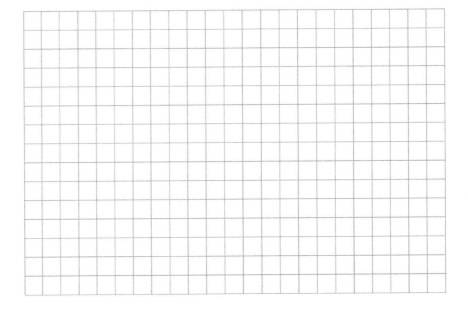

Acids and Bases

The reactivity of acids and bases are based on their ionization properties. Acid–base indicators help to differentiate acids and bases, and titrations can be used to find concentration amounts. Add to this graphic organizer to create study notes.

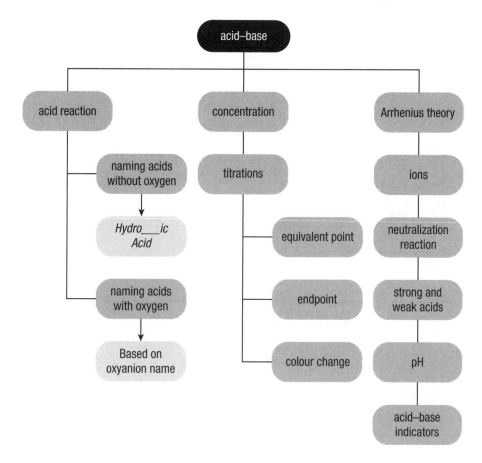

K/U Knowledge/Understanding
T/I Thinking/Investigation
C Communication
A Application

1. An acid that completely ionizes in water is a _____ acid. (10.2) K/U

2. Is the following statement true or false? If you think the statement is false, rewrite it to make it true: Hydroxide ions give acids their characteristics. (10.2) K/U

3. How can you determine if a compound is an acid just by looking at its chemical formula? K/U (10.1)

4. Fill in **Table 1** with the missing information. (10.1) C

Table 1 Acids That Do Not Contain Oxygen

Acid name	Chemical formula (aq)
	HCl
	H_2S
hydrofluoric acid	

5. Explain why chemists use two different systems to name acids. (10.2) K/U

6. According to the Arrhenius theory, when electrolytes dissolve, its ions _____. (10.2) K/U

7. Write the neutralization of phosphoric acid, H_3PO_4, and sodium hydroxide, NaOH. T/I (10.2)

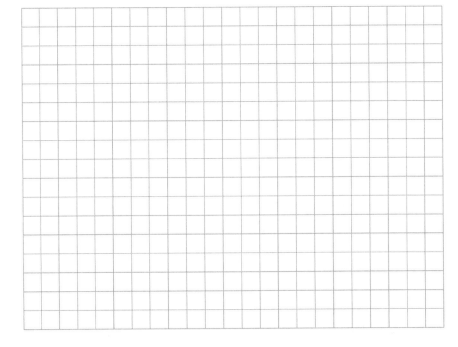

8. In order for a titration to give accurate results, what must happen? (10.3) K/U T/I

9. Titrations require _____ solutions. (10.3) K/U

10. You are performing a titration and you get a colour change. However, you want to make sure that the endpoint has been reached. What should you do? (10.3) K/U T/I

11. A 0.450 g mass of acetic acid, CH_3COOH, is dissolved in 0.500 L of water. The solution titrated with a sodium hydroxide, NaOH, solution of unknown concentration. It is determined that 0.400 L of the sodium hydroxide solution is needed to titrate the acetic acid. Calculate the amount concentration of the sodium hydroxide solution. The molar mass of acetic acid is 60.06 g/mol. (10.3) T/I

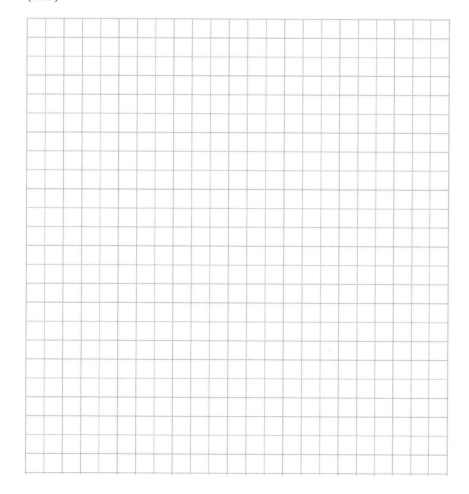

K/U Knowledge/Understanding
T/I Thinking/Investigation
C   Communication
A   Application

1. A solution of known concentration is a _____. (8.6) K/U
   (a) standard solution
   (b) primary solution
   (c) weak solution
   (d) acid

2. The chemical change that occurs in a reaction involving ions is a
   _____. (9.1) K/U
   (a) net ionic equation
   (b) spectator ion
   (c) formula equation
   (d) acid equation

3. Is the following statement true or false? If you think the statement is false, rewrite it to make it true: Transpiration describes the movement of water on, above, and below Earth's surface. (8.1) K/U

4. Hydrocarbons do not mix with water. Explain why. (8.3) K/U

5. Write a chemical equation for the dissociation of potassium chloride, KCl. (8.3) C

6. Label the area in **Figure 1** where a solution would be considered a supersaturated and an unsaturated solution. Explain. (8.5) C

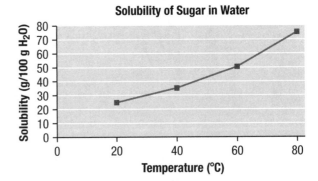

Figure 1

7. What is the amount concentration of a silver nitrate solution that contains 0.500 L of 45 g of silver nitrate, $AgNO_3$? The molar mass of $AgNO_3 = 169.88$ g/mol. (8.6) **C**

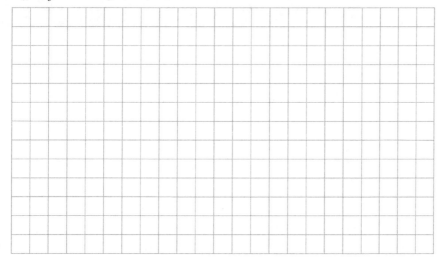

8. When doing a dilution, how do you decrease the concentration? (8.7) **K/U**

9. Write the formula equation for the reaction that occurs between silver and copper(II) chloride, $CuCl_2$. (9.1) **C**

10. Describe the difference between a quantitative and a qualitative test. (9.2) **K/U**

11. Write the chemical name for H_3PO_4 (aq). (10.1) **C**

12. Complete **Table 1** below that shows three anions and three formulas of anions for chlorine, Cl^-. (10.1) **C**

Table 1 Anions and Formulas

Anion	Formula of anion

13. Explain Arrhenius's theory in your own words. (10.2) **K/U** **C**

14. Name two characteristics that a primary standard should have when used in a titration. (10.3) **K/U**

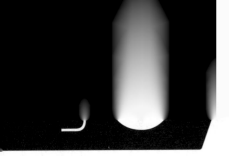

Chapter 11: The Gas State and Gas Laws

There are three common states of matter: solid, liquid, and gas. These three states have different properties, such as the ability to flow or to be compressed. The kinetic molecular theory (KMT) states that all substances contain entities that are in constant, random motion.

The atmosphere is a mixture of gases, liquids, and suspended solids, and is responsible for stabilizing the temperature of Earth, which prevents large extremes in daytime and nighttime temperatures from occurring. This is accomplished through the greenhouse effect, a naturally occurring process. Excess greenhouse gases in the atmosphere are the primary cause of climate change. Pollution can have a detrimental impact on human health. Air quality tools are used to measure pollution levels and the risk of air pollution to human health.

Gases behave in a specific manner that has been described through the gas laws. These laws include Charles' law: $\dfrac{V_1}{T_1} = \dfrac{V_2}{T_2}$; Boyle's law: $P_1V_1 = P_2V_2$; and Gay-Lussac's Law: $\dfrac{P_1}{T_1} = \dfrac{P_2}{T_2}$. These can be combined to give the combined gas law: $\dfrac{P_1V_1}{T_1} = \dfrac{P_2V_2}{T_2}$. The gas laws predict the behaviour of gases at particular temperatures and pressures.

BIG IDEAS

- Properties of gases can be described qualitatively and quantitatively, and can be predicted.
- Air quality can be affected by human activities and technology.
- People have a responsibility to protect the integrity of Earth's atmosphere.

Chapter 12: Gas Laws, Gas Mixtures, and Gas Reactions

Avogadro's law states that the volume of a gas is directly related to the amount of gas when temperature and pressure are constant. Equal volumes of gas under identical conditions contain the same number of entities. Mathematically, Avogadro's law is represented by $\dfrac{V_1}{n_1} = \dfrac{V_2}{n_2}$.

Avogadro's law, when combined with Boyle's law and Charles' law, produces the ideal gas law: $PV = nRT$. The ideal gas law states that the product of the pressure and volume of a gas is equal to the amount of gas, the universal gas constant, and the temperature. Mathematically, this formula is $PV = nRT$, where R is the universal gas constant and equal to $8.314 \cdot kPa \cdot L \cdot mol^{-1} \cdot K^{-1}$.

In the atmosphere and in the real world, gases are often in mixtures. Therefore, it is necessary to determine the properties of individual gases in mixtures. Pressure of gas mixtures can be measured using Dalton's law of partial pressure. Dalton's law of partial pressures states that the total pressure of a mixture of non-reacting gases is equal to the sum of the partial pressures of the individual gases. This is represented mathematically as $P_{total} = P_1 + P_2 + P_3 + \ldots$

States of Matter and the Kinetic Molecular Theory

Textbook pp. 516–519

Vocabulary

Brownian motion   kinetic molecular theory   kinetic energy   temperature

MAIN IDEA: Matter exists in three common states: solid, liquid, and gas. These states of matter have unique properties that are shaped by the attractions between molecules and the motion of the molecules.

1. Complete the concept map (**Figure 1**), describing three properties for each state of matter. K/U C

STUDY TIP

Visualize It
Solids, liquids, and gases have specific properties that distinguish them from each other. Molecules in a solid are very close together. Molecules in a gas are farther apart but not widely spread apart. Molecules in a gas have great distances between them.

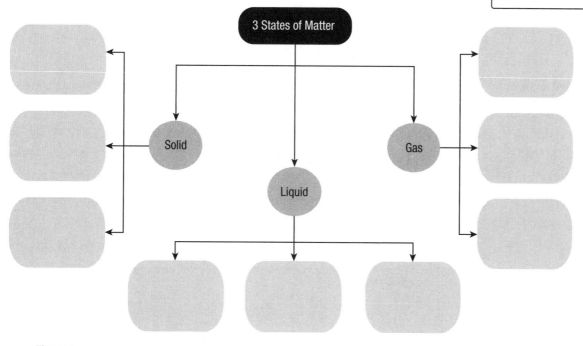

Figure 1

2. Why are solids difficult to compress? K/U

3. Why can you smell a skunk's odour when driving in a car? [T/I] [A]

4. (a) What is Brownian motion? [K/U]

   (b) Brownian motion led to the development of kinetic molecular theory (KMT). Describe KMT. [K/U]

5. _____ is the energy of an entity due to its motion. [K/U]
   (a) Potential energy
   (b) Kinetic energy
   (c) Random energy
   (d) Real energy

6. Complete **Table 1** below by identifying two properties of each type of motion. [K/U]

Table 1 Properties of the Three Types of Motion

Type of Motion	Properties
translational motion	1. 2.
rotational motion	1. 2.
vibrational motion	1. 2.

7. Is the following statement true or false? If you think the statement is false, rewrite it to make it true: Solids have vibrational and rotational motion and the weakest strength of attraction between molecules. [K/U]

8. What happens to the molecules in a gas when they are heated? K/U

9. Identify the state of matter of each substance described below. Then explain how you know. K/U T/I
   (a) The substance is heated, and the molecules vibrate faster but do not move farther apart.

   (b) The substance is heated and the vibrational, rotational, and translational motion increases. The substance expands to the size of the room.

MAIN IDEA: Temperature affects the distance between molecules and the motion of the molecules, causing a change in the state of matter.

10. _____ is the measure of the average kinetic energy of the entities in a substance. K/U
    (a) Potential energy
    (b) Mass
    (c) Temperature
    (d) Volume

11. As a substance is heated, its molecules move faster and become farther apart. When this occurs in a liquid, the liquid may change into a gas. This is known as _____. K/U

12. An ice cube is heated to 100 °C. K/U
    (a) Describe what happens to the molecules.

    (b) What happens to the ice?

> **STUDY TIP**
>
> **Consider Temperature**
> Think about times when you have heated water or put an ice cube in a glass of water. When thermal energy is applied, think about how the molecules are moving and how they react to a change in temperature.

The Atmosphere and Its Components

> **Vocabulary**
>
> greenhouse effect   carbon sequestration

MAIN IDEA: The atmosphere plays an important role in sustaining life on Earth. The atmosphere has four layers: troposphere, stratosphere, mesosphere, and thermosphere.

1. Most of the gases in the atmosphere are concentrated in the first
   _____ above Earth's surface. **K/U**
   (a) 10 km
   (b) 100 km
   (c) 1000 km
   (d) 100 cm

2. Is the following statement true or false? If you think the statement is false, rewrite it to make it true: The mesosphere is denser than the stratosphere. **K/U**

3. Is the oxygen concentration higher in the thermosphere or the stratosphere? Explain. **T/I**

4. Air movements in the _____ determine weather patterns. **K/U**
   (a) stratosphere
   (b) thermosphere
   (c) mesosphere
   (d) troposphere

5. As altitude increases, the temperature of the atmosphere typically decreases. This does not occur in the stratosphere. Why? **T/I**

6. Complete the graphic organizer below (**Figure 1**), noting two properties for each of the four layers of the atmosphere. K/U C

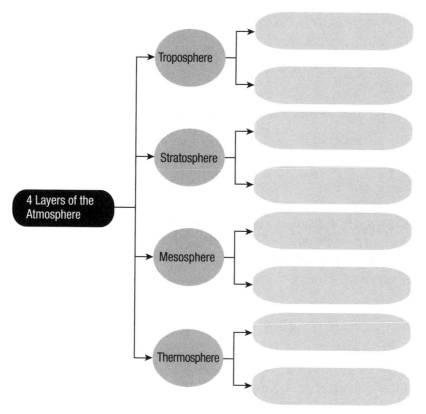

Figure 1

7. Auroras are natural light displays that appear over the polar regions. What causes this phenomenon to occur? T/I

8. Nitrogen-fixing bacteria convert nitrogen gas from the atmosphere into gas soluble nitrates. K/U T/I A

   (a) This process is part of the _____ cycle.

   (b) Why is this process important to sustaining human life on Earth?

   (c) How does plant decay contribute to the nitrogen cycle?

9. Ozone in the stratosphere is being depleted. Why is this a cause for alarm? [K/U] [T/I]

10. Why is carbon dioxide so important to plants? [K/U]

MAIN IDEA: The atmosphere stabilizes Earth's temperature through the greenhouse effect. Increased concentrations of greenhouse gases in the atmosphere have contributed to climate change. Climate change is having a significant effect on Earth.

11. Explain in your own words the greenhouse effect. [K/U] [C]

12. Is the following statement true or false? If you think the statement is false, rewrite it to make it true: The greater the concentration of greenhouse gases in the atmosphere, the greater the greenhouse effect. [K/U]

13. Fill in **Table 1** to describe some of the effects of climate change. [T/I]

Table 1 Effects of Climate Change

Effect of climate change	Risk
sea levels rise	flooding in coastal areas
changes in mean temperature	

14. Carbon sequestration is the process of capturing and storing carbon dioxide. Complete **Table 2** to summarize what you know about carbon sequestration. [K/U] [C]

Table 2 Common Types of Carbon Sequestration

Type of sequestration	Example of a strategy	Major benefits or risks

The Road to Discovering Argon

Textbook pp. 526–527

MAIN IDEA: Determining the identity of a substance that is invisible, odourless, and rarely reacts is a difficult challenge. Sometimes discoveries in science are made by chance. This is what happened when argon was discovered.

1. Argon is a noble gas. What does that mean in terms of its reactivity? T/I

2. (a) Give examples of two other noble gases.

   (b) Why are noble gases important? K/U

3. In his experiment, Rayleigh believed that if he removed oxygen from air, pure nitrogen would remain. Why did Rayleigh make this hypothesis? K/U

4. How did chemist Sir William Ramsay finally solve the mystery of the unknown gas in the atmosphere? K/U

5. Why was the discovery of argon such a challenge to chemists? K/U

6. Why was the discovery of argon so important to the development of the periodic table? K/U

Air Quality

Textbook pp. 528–533

Vocabulary		
photochemical smog	particulate matter	Air Quality Health Index (AQHI)

MAIN IDEA: Pollution released into the air can cause chemical reactions that create further health and environmental hazards.

1. Fill in **Table 1** to describe photochemical smog. K/U C

Table 1 Photochemical Smog

definition	
composition	
where it comes from	
appearance	
impact on human health	

2. _____ is a mixture of solid and liquid particles found in the atmosphere. K/U

3. Most combustion reactions result in the production of particulate matter. Name three activities that may contribute to the release of particulate matter into the environment. T/I

4. Sulfur, when it is burned, is transformed into sulfur dioxide, SO_2, a pollutant gas. Fill in **Table 2** to describe sulfur dioxide. K/U C

Table 2 Sulfur Dioxide

balanced equation for the burning of sulfur in oxygen	
physical properties	
impact on environment	

5. Why is the concentration of carbon monoxide higher in urban areas? A

6. Carbon monoxide is produced during _____ combustion. K/U

7. Is the following statement true or false? If you think the statement is false, rewrite it to make it true: Particulate matter includes carbon-containing compounds that vaporize readily. K/U

8. Atmospheric ozone provides crucial protection from the ultraviolet rays from the Sun. Ground level ozone, however, can be harmful to human health. K/U T/I A

   (a) How is ground level ozone produced?

   (b) Why is the concentration of ground level ozone highest on sunny days?

   (c) How can using public transportation reduce the amount of ground level ozone that is present?

MAIN IDEA: Air pollution has become a significant threat to human health. Environment Canada has developed alert tools such as the Air Quality Health Index (AQHI) to measure the health risks associated with air quality (**Figure 1**).

Figure 1

9. The weather report says that the AQHI is at 8 today. You are scheduled to play a soccer game outside at 4 p.m. Would you still play? Why or why not? T/I A

Indoor Air Quality

Vocabulary
off-gassing

MAIN IDEA: Air indoors is two to five times more polluted than the air outdoors. Indoor pollutants can come from chemical or biological sources. Chemical sources of indoor pollutants include gases and particles.

1. List three sources of indoor chemical pollutants. K/U

    (i)

    (ii)

    (iii)

2. _____ is the release of gases from a substance at room temperature. K/U

3. Is the following statement true or false? If you think the statement is false, rewrite it to make it true: Off-gassed chemicals are usually greenhouse gases that evaporate into the air at room temperature. K/U

4. The smell of a freshly painted room is unique. Over time, the smell dissipates. Why? K/U T/I

5. Methanal is a common volatile organic compound that can be off-gassed in the home. Fill in **Table 1** to describe its properties. K/U C

Table 1 Methanal

products from which methanal can be off-gassed	
health risks	
ways to minimize exposure to methanal at home	

6. Carbon monoxide poisoning occurs when hemoglobin is not able to uptake oxygen in the lungs. Fill in the flow chart (**Figure 1**) to show what happens during carbon monoxide poisoning. K/U C

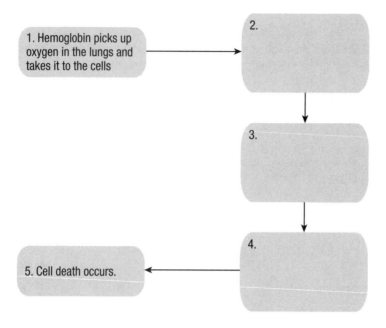

1. Hemoglobin picks up oxygen in the lungs and takes it to the cells

2.

3.

4.

5. Cell death occurs.

Figure 1

7. List some of the symptoms of carbon monoxide poisoning. Classify them as mild, moderate, or severe. K/U T/I

mild symptoms:

moderate symptoms:

severe symptoms:

8. Write a balanced combustion reaction in which methane, $CH_4(g)$, reacts with oxygen to produce carbon monoxide and water. C A

9. _____ is the leading cause of lung cancer among non-smokers. K/U

MAIN IDEA: Biological pollutants are also commonly found indoors. Biological pollutants include microscopic organisms and contaminants produced by living organisms.

10. How could your pet be considered a source of indoor pollution? K/U A

11. Biological contaminants thrive in conditions of _____ humidity. K/U

Car Idling

Textbook pp. 539–540

MAIN IDEA: Maintaining good air quality is an important issue for maintaining human and animal health. Even simple acts like car idling can contribute significantly to poor air quality.

1. Name three toxic airborne chemicals that are produced from car exhaust. K/U

2. Using your answers to Question 1, complete the cause–effect graphic organizer below (**Figure 1**). K/U C

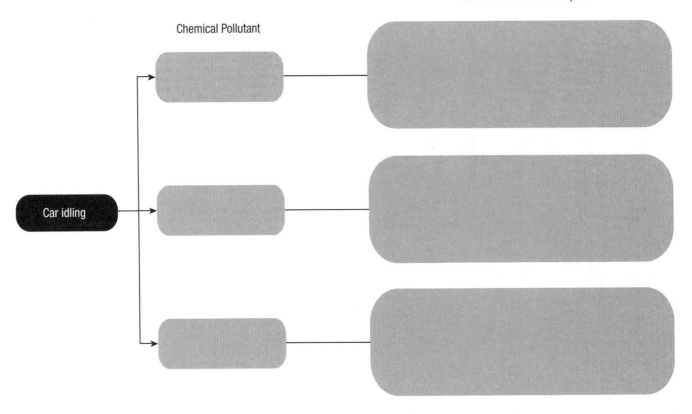

Figure 1

3. Why does an idling engine produce such a large amount of pollutants as compared to a car running at 60 km/h? K/U T/I

4. Why are children at a higher risk for developing health problems related to poor air quality? K/U T/I

Atmospheric Pressure

Textbook pp. 541–546

Vocabulary

pressure (P)	standard	standard temperature	standard ambient temperature
atmospheric	pressure	and pressure (STP)	and pressure (SATP)
pressure			

MAIN IDEA: The force of gravity pulls the atmosphere down on us, creating this force. Pressure (P) is defined as the force (F) exerted per unit area (A).

$$P = \frac{F}{A}$$

1. What is the SI unit for pressure? **K/U**
   (a) degrees Celsius
   (b) the Pascal
   (c) the Newton
   (d) Avogadro's number

2. Is the following statement true or false? If you think the statement is false, rewrite it to make it true: Pressure is directly related to the temperature applied. **K/U**

3. If the same force is applied to a small area and a large area, which area will have the greater pressure? Explain. **K/U**

MAIN IDEA: Atmospheric pressure is the force per unit area exerted by air on all objects.

4. (a) Standard air pressure is about _____. **K/U**
   (b) Standard air pressure is also measured in _____. **K/U**

5. Explain the difference between standard temperature and pressure (STP) and standard ambient temperature and pressure (SATP).

6. Convert 0.875 atm to mm Hg.

> **STUDY TIP**
>
> **Standard Air Pressure**
> Although air pressure is all around us, we do not feel it. This is because our bodies maintain an internal pressure that matches the outside pressure and pushes back against standard air pressure. When external air pressure increases, we can feel the impact on our bodies.

> **STUDY TIP**
>
> **Pressure on an Airplane**
> In order to fly, airlines must pressurize their cabins. Pressurization of the cabin prevents the atmospheric pressure from crushing the aircraft as it ascends into the atmosphere.

7. Why do some climbers on Mt. Everest require oxygen tanks? K/U A

8. Is the following statement true or false? If you think the statement is false, rewrite it to make it true: The density of atmospheric gases is greatest above sea level. K/U

9. Consider a general helium tank when answering the questions below. T/I
   (a) If standard atmospheric pressure pushing on the tank is 101 kPa, why does the cylinder not collapse?

   (b) Suppose that air pressure on the outside of the tank increased. What would happen to the tank?

   (c) What would happen if the pressure inside the tank increased above that of the external atmospheric pressure?

10. High altitude training is used by some athletes to improve performance. How does high altitude training affect the body? K/U T/I

The Gas Laws—Absolute Temperature and Charles' Law

Textbook pp. 547–553

> **Vocabulary**
>
> absolute zero   Kelvin temperature scale   absolute temperature   Charles' Law

MAIN IDEA: The Celsius, or centigrade, scale was developed to measure temperature in everyday situations. The Kelvin temperature scale is based on absolute zero, the temperature at which a gas theoretically has no volume.

1. When the volume of a gas reaches zero, it approaches absolute zero or _____ degrees Celsius.

2. Is the following statement true or false? If you think the statement is false, rewrite it to make it true: At absolute zero, there is no potential energy in the gas and therefore no thermal energy. K/U

> **LEARNING TIP**
>
> **°C vs. K**
> Note that the unit for centigrade is degree Celsius (°C), whereas the unit for absolute temperature is Kelvin (K). There is no degree symbol.

3. Express 50 °C as an absolute temperature. T/I

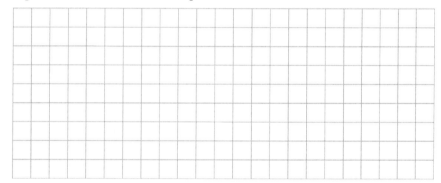

MAIN IDEA: Charles' Law states that the volume of a gas is directly proportional to its temperature in kelvins, provided the pressure and amount of gas are constant. This is represented by

$$V = aT \quad \text{or} \quad \frac{V_1}{T_1} = \frac{V_2}{T_2}$$

4. (a) According to Charles' Law, if absolute temperature is doubled, what will happen to the volume of the gas? K/U

   (b) If the Celsius scale is used, will the same result occur? K/U

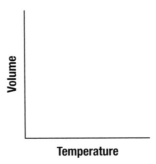
5. Apply Charles' Law to complete the following flow chart (**Figure 1**). K/U A

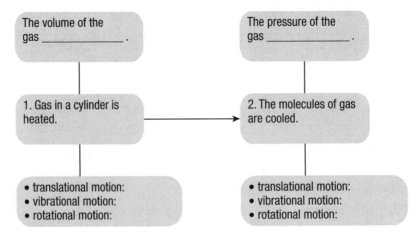

The volume of the gas _____ .

The pressure of the gas _____ .

1. Gas in a cylinder is heated.

2. The molecules of gas are cooled.

- translational motion:
- vibrational motion:
- rotational motion:

- translational motion:
- vibrational motion:
- rotational motion:

Figure 1

6. On **Figure 2**, graph the relationship between temperature and volume.

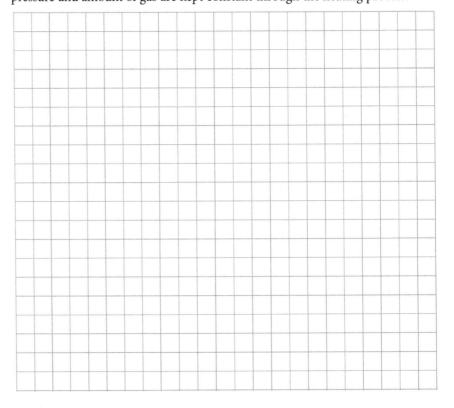

Figure 2

7. A 0.410 L sample of argon is collected at 45 °C. If the temperature of the sample is increased to 75 °C, what volume will the gas occupy? Assume that the pressure and amount of gas are kept constant through the heating process. T/I

The Gas Laws—Boyle's Law, Gay-Lussac's Law, and the Combined Gas Law

Textbook pp. 554–562

Boyle's law   Gay-Lussac's law   combined gas law

MAIN IDEA: As the volume of a gas decreases, its pressure increases. This is known as Boyle's law.

$$P_1V_1 = P_2V_2 \quad \text{or} \quad PV = \text{constant}$$

1. When you inhale, the volume of your lungs increases. When the volume of your lungs increases, the pressure in your lungs _____. K/U

2. According to Boyle's law, pressure is _____ related to volume. K/U
   (a) inversely
   (b) directly
   (c) proportionally
   (d) not

3. Is the following statement true or false? If you think the statement is false, rewrite it to make it true: When helium gas is released from a tank into a balloon, the volume of the balloon increases. This means that the pressure of the helium increases as well. K/U

Inverse Relationship
When one variable is changed (increased or decreased) and the other responds in the opposite manner, the two variables are inversely related (or inversely proportional) to each other. As a real-world example, as the number of people buying tickets to a concert increases, the number of available seats decreases. These variables are inversely proportional.

4. As the volume of a gas decreases, its pressure increases. Explain what happens to the motion of the molecules in the gas. K/U

5. Assume that a gas fills a 0.55 L container at 1.0 kPa. If the volume of the gas is increased to 4.0 L, what will be the pressure of the gas?

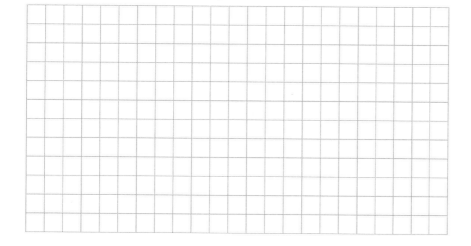

Think About It
As you apply the gas laws, think about pressure, temperature, and volume in a real-world setting. Based on the data given, you should be able to make a prediction about the variable that you are seeking. Check your answer to see if it makes sense and compares with your real-world example.

MAIN IDEA: Gay-Lussac's law states that the pressure of a gas increases as the temperature increases. This is represented mathematically by the formula

$$\frac{P_1}{T_1} = \frac{P_2}{T_2} \quad \text{or} \quad \frac{P}{T} = \text{constant}$$

6. When a balloon is brought from inside a warm house out into the cold, it shrinks. Why does this happen? T/I A

7. Gay-Lussac's law states that as the pressure of a gas increases, the temperature increases _____. K/U
   (a) inversely
   (b) exponentially
   (c) proportionally
   (d) inappropriately

8. Is the following statement true or false? If you think the statement is false, rewrite it to make it true: When the temperature of a gas increases, its pressure will decrease. K/U

9. An increase in the temperature of a gas will increase its _____ energy. K/U

10. Assume that a gas is at room temperature 25 °C and 1.0 Pa of pressure in a standard cylinder. If the temperature of the gas is increased to 75 °C, what will be the final pressure of the gas? A

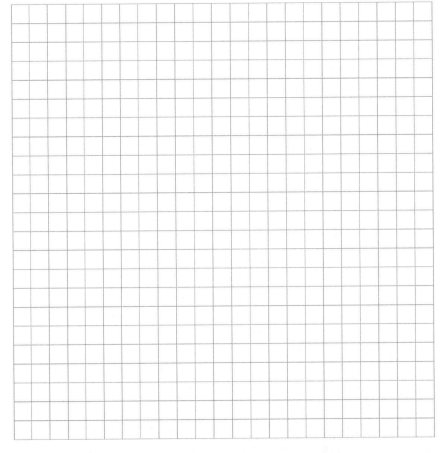

LEARNING TIP

Mathematical Mess
As you rearrange the combined gas law, things can get messy quickly. Be sure to take one step at a time and be careful as you perform mathematical operations. Do a quick check to make sure you rearranged the equation correctly. If you include the units in the rearranged equation, you should be left with the correct units after the others have cancelled out.

MAIN IDEA: Charles' law, Boyle's law, and Gay-Lussac's law can be combined so that changes in pressure, temperature, and volume can all be taken into account when evaluating a gas. This law is known as the combined gas law.

$$\frac{P_1 V_1}{T_1} = \frac{P_2 V_2}{T_2} \quad \text{or} \quad \frac{PV}{T} = \text{constant}$$

11. The product of the pressure and volume of a gas divided by its absolute temperature is constant as long as _____. K/U

   (a) the external environment does not change

   (b) the atmospheric pressure does not change

   (c) the amount of the gas remains constant

   (d) temperature decreases

12. A gas is placed in a cylinder and has a pressure of 33.3 kPa, a temperature of 25 °C, and a volume of 0.345 L. The pressure of the gas is increased to 40 kPa, and the volume is increased to 0.50 L. What is the temperature of the gas? T/I

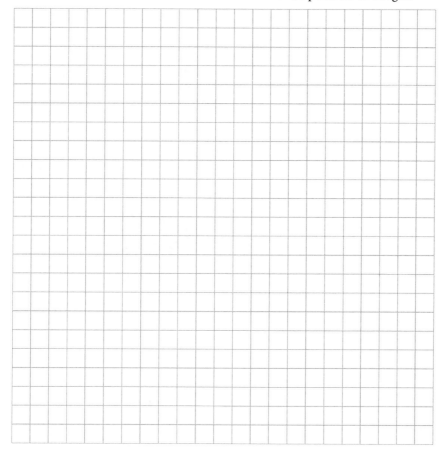

The Gas State and Gas Laws

Survival on Earth is possible because of the atmosphere. The atmosphere is comprised mostly of gases. Given the importance of gases in the atmosphere, it is essential to understand how these substances behave. The following graphic organizer summarizes some of the main ideas from Chapter 11. Add to it to create your own study notes.

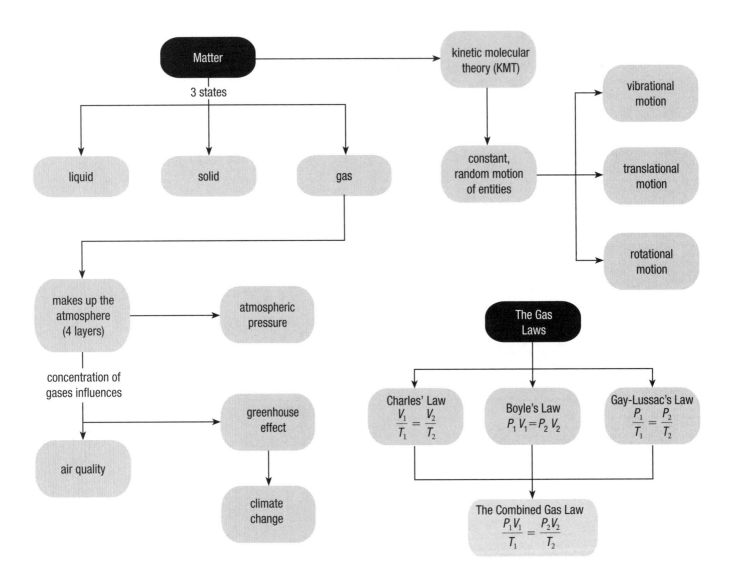

1. It has a definite shape and volume, is virtually incompressible, and does not flow easily. What state of matter is being described? (11.1) **K/U**
   - (a) liquid
   - (b) solid
   - (c) gas
   - (d) none of the above

2. What type of motion is the movement of an entity through space along a linear path (straight line)? (11.1) **K/U**
   - (a) vibrational
   - (b) rotational
   - (c) kinetic
   - (d) translational

3. Is each of the following statements true or false? If you think the statement is false, rewrite it to make it true. **K/U**
   - (a) Boyle's law states that entities in solids, liquids, and gases are in constant, random motion. (11.1, 11.8)

   - (b) As more energy is transferred to a solid, its molecules will vibrate faster. (11.1)

4. The atmosphere is comprised of four layers: the troposphere, the _____, the _____, and the _____. (11.2) **K/U**

5. Explain what happens to molecules when a gas cools. (11.1) **K/U**

6. Complete the graphic organizer (**Figure 1**), showing how Charles' law, Boyle's law, and Gay-Lussac's law contribute to the combined gas law. (11.8, 11.9) **K/U** **C**

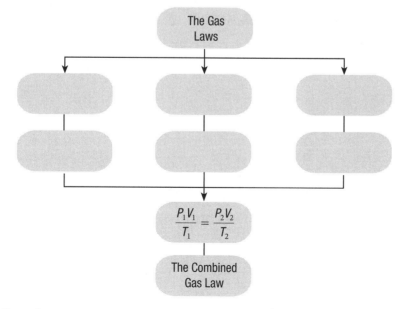

Figure 1

7. **Figure 2** provides a review of the greenhouse effect. Explain what is occurring at points A, B, and C. (11.2) C A

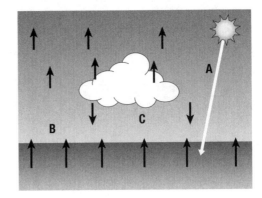

Figure 2 The greenhouse effect

A. _____

_____

B. _____

_____

C. _____

_____

8. The gas shown in **Figure 3** has decreased in volume. (11.9) K/U A

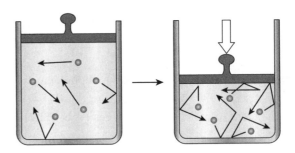

Figure 3

(a) What gas law is being illustrated?

(b) What happens to the molecules when the volume is decreased?

Avogadro's Law and Molar Volume

Textbook pp. 576–581

Vocabulary

law of combining volumes   Avogadro's Law   molar volume

MAIN IDEA: Gas laws including Charles' law, Boyle's law, Gay-Lussac's law, and the combined gas law assume that the amount of gas in a sample remains constant. If we want to change the amount of the gas, additional tools are needed. The law of combining volumes states that when measured at the same temperature and pressure, volumes of gaseous reactions are always in simple ratios of whole numbers.

1. The law of combining volumes can only be applied to which of the following? K/U
   (a) solids
   (b) gases
   (c) liquids
   (d) electrical currents

2. The law of combining volumes indicates that volumes are always in simple ratios. Determine the ratio for each reaction in **Table 1** below. T/I

   Table 1 Reactions and Ratios

Reaction	Ratio
$2H_2 + O_2 \longrightarrow 2H_2O$	
$H_2 + Cl_2 \longrightarrow 2HCl$	
$N_2 + 3H_2 \longrightarrow 2NH_3$	

STUDY TIP

Consider the Gas Laws
Charles' law, Boyle's law, and Gay-Lussac's law all show important relationships between variables related to gases. Consider these relationships as you explore the law of combining volumes and Avogadro's law.

MAIN IDEA: Avogadro's law states that the volume of a gas is directly related to the amount of gas when temperature and pressure are constant. Equal volumes of gas under identical conditions contain the same number of entities. Mathematically, Avogadro's law is represented by

$$\frac{V_1}{n_1} = \frac{V_2}{n_2}$$

3. The coefficients in the chemical equations in **Table 1** also correspond to the _____ ratio and _____ ratio of products and reactants. K/U

4. Explain in your own words how the amount of gas can be increased if pressure and temperature are kept constant. C

LEARNING TIP

Thought Experiment
A "thought experiment" is a way to solve a problem using your imagination. In a thought experiment, instead of carrying out an actual experiment, you imagine the practical outcome.

STUDY TIP

Visualize It
Visualize the relationships between volume, pressure, temperature, and moles by picturing a balloon. What happens to the balloon as certain variables change or are held constant? By visualizing it, you may be able to better understand how one variable impacts another.

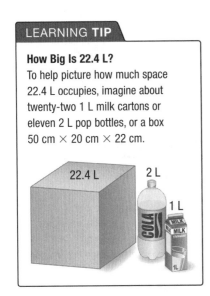

Figure 1

5. **Figure 1** shows two containers that have both gas molecules and empty space. Refer to **Figure 1** and Avogadro's law to complete the graphic organizer (**Figure 2**). K/U C A

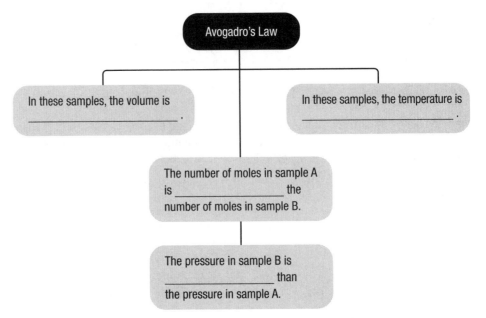

Avogadro's Law

In these samples, the volume is _____ .

In these samples, the temperature is _____ .

The number of moles in sample A is _____ the number of moles in sample B.

The pressure in sample B is _____ than the pressure in sample A.

Figure 2

LEARNING TIP

How Big Is 22.4 L?
To help picture how much space 22.4 L occupies, imagine about twenty-two 1 L milk cartons or eleven 2 L pop bottles, or a box 50 cm × 20 cm × 22 cm.

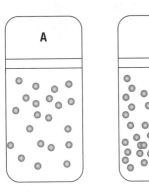

6. A cylinder with a piston contains 2.00 g of helium at constant temperature and pressure. More helium is added to the cylinder and the piston is adjusted so that the pressure remains constant. How many grams of helium were added to the cylinder if the volume changed from 2.00 L to 2.70 L? T/I

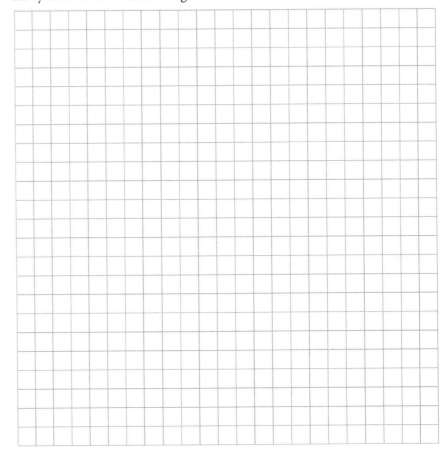

MAIN IDEA: The molar volume of a gas is the volume that one mole of a gas occupies at a specific temperature and pressure.

7. Is the following statement true or false? If you think the statement is false, rewrite it to make it true: If one mole of hydrogen gas and one mole of oxygen gas are under the same pressure and at the same temperature, they will occupy different volumes. K/U

8. One mole of any ideal gas at standard temperature and pressure will occupy what volume? K/U
   (a) 22.4 L
   (b) 24.8 L
   (c) 1.0 L
   (d) The volume cannot be determined.

Ideal Gases and the Ideal Gas Law

Textbook pp. 582–589

MAIN IDEA: Gas laws including Charles' law, Boyle's law, Gay-Lussac's law, and Avogadro's law are based on the idea that gases behave ideally. Ideal gases are composed of particles that have zero size, travel in straight lines, and have no attractions to each other.

1. Is the following statement true or false? If you think the statement is false, rewrite it to make it true: In reality, there are no ideal gases. K/U

2. Complete the bubble map below (**Figure 1**), identifying the properties of an ideal gas. K/U

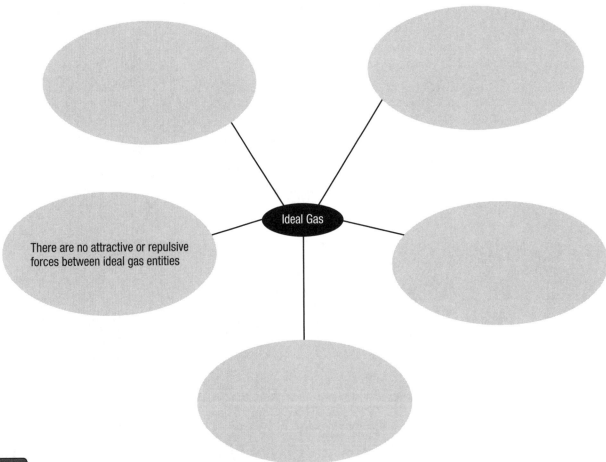

Figure 1

3. When ideal gases collide with the walls of a container, these collisions are said to be elastic. What does this mean? K/U

STUDY TIP

The Ideal Gas Law
The ideal gas law provides solutions for one set of data. Gas laws including Charles' law, Boyle's law, Gay-Lussac's law and Avogadro's law require two sets of data.

MAIN IDEA: The ideal gas law states that the product of the pressure and volume of a gas is equal to the amount of gas, the universal gas constant, and the temperature. Mathematically, this formula is $PV = nRT$, where R is the universal gas constant and equal to 8.314 kPa • L • mol^{-1} • K^{-1}.

4. A sample of 10.0 g of methane has a volume of 5.0 L at 25 °C. Calculate the pressure of the gas. T/I

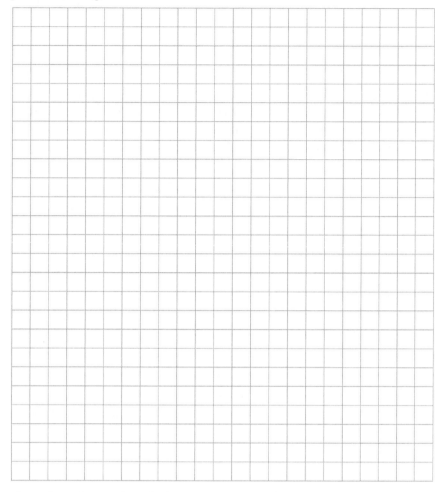

LEARNING TIP

R and the Ideal Gas Law
Look closely at the units of R and you will see that they represent the variables in the ideal gas law: "kPa" for pressure, "L" for volume, and so on.

5. The molar volume of an ideal gas is 22.414 L/mol at STP. Measurements of gases such as helium and chlorine demonstrate, however, that molar volumes are different, 22.436 L and 22.063 L, respectively. Why is this so? K/U

6. When a gas is placed under high pressure and low temperature, how will the motion of gas molecules compare to the motion of ideal gas molecules? K/U
   (a) It will deviate insignificantly.
   (b) It will not deviate.
   (c) It will deviate significantly.
   (d) It will increase proportionately.

7. Is the following statement true or false? If you think the statement is false, rewrite it to make it true: Real gases do not condense into solids or liquids. K/U

8. Nitrogen gas can be cooled and compressed into a liquid. Explain how this can happen based on your understanding of the properties of real gases. `T/I`

9. Gases have distinct properties that are affected by temperature and pressure. Using the compare and contrast chart below (**Figure 2**), identify the properties of a gas at normal pressure and at high pressure, as well as the properties of a gas at normal temperature and at high temperature. `K/U` `A`

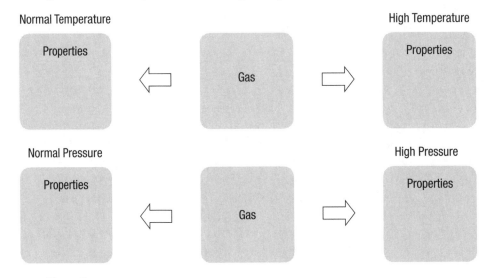

Figure 2

The Science of Cold

Textbook pp. 590–591

MAIN IDEA: Understanding the science of cold has been and continues to be a remarkable scientific process. Although we may not think much about it, the science of cold is unique and required extensive exploration to discover.

1. What discovery opened the floodgates in cold research? K/U

2. (a) Based on what you know about the gas laws, what happens to the molecules in a gas when the temperature and pressure are lowered? K/U

   (b) How do these changes result in a state change for the gas, that is, liquefying the gas? K/U

> **STUDY TIP**
>
> **Liquid Nitrogen**
> Liquid nitrogen is an example of a gas that has been liquefied. When it is exposed to normal room temperature and pressure conditions, it becomes a gas very rapidly. Containers with liquid nitrogen inside must be cooled slowly to prevent them from exploding. This type of explosion is similar to what occurred in Kamerlingh Onnes' laboratory.

3. The Bose–Einstein condensate was a unique state of matter. K/U T/I
   (a) What occurred in this state of matter?

   (b) How did researchers at the University of Colorado make the Bose-Einstein condensate?

4. The discovery of cold continues today. K/U
   (a) What does this suggest about scientific research?

   (b) What does this mean in terms of the importance of collaboration in research?

Gas Mixtures and the Law of Partial Pressures

Textbook pp. 592–597

Vocabulary

partial pressure   Dalton's law of partial pressures

MAIN IDEA: Most naturally occurring gases are mixtures. As such, determining the properties of a mixture of gases provides a more practical application for understanding gases and their behaviour.

1. Through his research, scientist John Dalton found that air at higher temperatures could hold _____ concentrations of water vapour than air at lower temperatures. [K/U]

   (a) lower

   (b) greater

   (c) similar

   (d) Air at high temperatures cannot hold water.

2. Is the following statement true or false? If you think the statement is false, rewrite it to make it true: When water vapour is added to dry air, the pressure of the air will decrease. [K/U]

3. Define partial pressure. [K/U]

> **STUDY TIP**
>
> **Consider the Air Around You**
> When you step outside on a humid day, the air is full of water vapour. You can feel this vapour against your skin. Water vapour is controlled by both temperature and pressure. This explains why humidity exists on a cold day and why low humidity may be present on a very hot day.

MAIN IDEA: Dalton's law of partial pressures states that the total pressure of a mixture of non-reacting gases is equal to the sum of the partial pressures of the individual gases.

$$P_{total} = P_1 + P_2 + P_3 + \dots$$

4. In order for Dalton's law to be applied, what two conditions must be met? [K/U]

   1.

   2.

5. How does kinetic molecular theory explain Dalton's law of partial pressures? [K/U] [A]

> **STUDY TIP**
>
> **Visualize What Happens**
> To understand Dalton's law of partial pressure, think about how molecules of two gases will respond when placed in the same container at constant temperature. The number of collisions between the gases and the container will increase, causing the pressure to increase.

---

6. A gas contains a mixture of nitrogen, helium, and oxygen at a total of 150 kPa. The pressure of the oxygen is 100 kPa, and the pressure of nitrogen is 34 kPa. What is the pressure of the helium? T/I

7. **Figure 1** shows water vapour molecules over a small pool of water. K/U

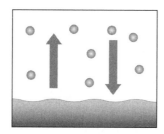

Figure 1

(a) When the temperature of the water is increased, the number of water vapour molecules in the air will _____.

(b) If the temperature increases, what will happen to the vapour pressure? Explain in terms of kinetic molecular theory.

8. Butane displaces water in a glass container over water. If the total pressure in the container is 65 kPa and the temperature is 19 °C, what is the partial pressure of the butane in the container? T/I

Reactions of Gases and Gas Stoichiometry

MAIN IDEA: Gases are involved in chemical reactions. These reactions are all around us. Gases interact with solids, liquids, and other gases. Using the reactions of gases, it is possible to predict their volume.

1. When working with reactions involving gases, _____ rather than mole ratios are used. K/U
   (a) volumes
   (b) grams
   (c) pressures
   (d) temperatures

2. Is the following statement true or false? If you think the statement is false, rewrite it to make it true: When gases react, the volumes of the reactants and the products react in whole number ratios if the temperature and pressure change. K/U

3. Gases react chemically with each other and with other forms of matter. These reactions are represented in _____. K/U
   (a) ratios
   (b) balanced chemical reactions
   (c) volumes
   (d) Avogadro's number

MAIN IDEA: The law of combining volumes for gas reactions states that the volumes of gaseous reactants and products of a chemical reaction are in simple ratios of whole numbers. These whole numbers can be used to solve simple gas stoichiometry problems.

4. Octane is burned in a car engine in the presence of oxygen producing carbon dioxide and water. T/I
   (a) Write a balanced equation for this reaction.

   (b) Use the law of combining volumes to predict the volume of oxygen required to burn 120 mL of octane in this engine.

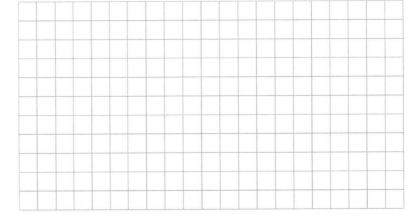

5. Is the following statement true or false? If you think the statement is false, rewrite it to make it true: If the mass of the reactants and temperature change during a reaction, the ideal gas law should be used to calculate the volume. **K/U**

6. Assume that 200.0 L of H_2 reacts at 25 °C and 88 kPa. How many litres of O_2 will be required to make H_2O at STP? **T/I**

Textbook p. 604

Burning Snowballs

MAIN IDEA: The limited amount of fossil fuels available for energy creation has prompted efforts to find new sources of energy. Gas hydrates may provide a viable alternative energy source for meeting human demand for energy. Even though gas hydrates have some unique benefits, these resources also have some important drawbacks that must be considered.

1. Is the following statement true or false? If you think the statement is false, rewrite it to make it true: Gas hydrates form under low temperatures and low pressures. K/U

2. Fill in **Table 1** with some benefits and drawbacks of using gas hydrates. K/U T/I C

Table 1 Benefits and Drawbacks of Gas Hydrates

Benefits	Drawbacks

3. Even though gas hydrates may provide a powerful energy source, burning these sources will still result in the release of greenhouses gases. What can be done to make this energy resource greener? T/I

4. Suppose you are asked to prepare a report on a specific fossil fuel alternative. What type of information should be included in the report? T/I A

Gas Laws, Gas Mixtures, and Gas Reactions

Gases react with one another, affecting their behaviour. Ideal gases provide a valuable tool for understanding the behaviour of gases. However, in practice, many of the properties of ideal gases are not maintained. The graphic organizer below summarizes some of the main ideas from Chapter 12. Add notes to create your own study notes.

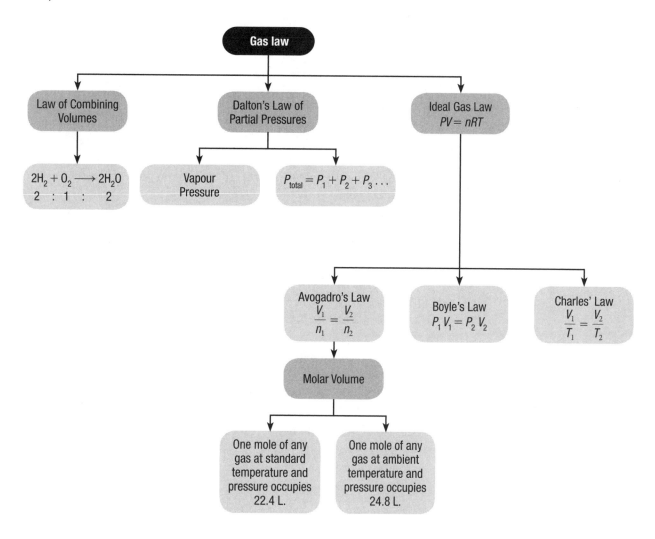

K/U   Knowledge/Understanding
T/I   Thinking/Investigation
C   Communication
A   Application

1. _____ states that when measured at the same temperature and pressure, volumes of gaseous reactants and products of chemical reactions are always in simple ratios of whole numbers. (12.1) K/U
   (a) The ideal gas law
   (b) The law of combining volumes
   (c) Avogadro's law
   (d) Dalton's law

2. Which of the following equations represents Avogadro's law? (12.1) K/U
   (a) $PV = nRT$
   (b) $\dfrac{V_1}{T_1} = \dfrac{V_2}{T_2}$
   (c) $P_1V_1 = P_2V_2$
   (d) $\dfrac{V_1}{n_1} = \dfrac{V_2}{n_2}$

3. Is each of the following statements true or false? If you think the statement is false, rewrite it to make it true. K/U
   (a) The volume of an ideal gas is significant when compared with the volume of the container. (12.2)

   (b) All liquids exist with a certain amount of vapour above their surface as a result of condensation. (12.4)

4. There are no attractive or repulsive forces between gas molecules. This statement refers to a(n) _____ gas. (12.2) K/U

5. When the actual molar volumes of real gases are examined, they differ from the standard 22.4 L. Why? (12.2) K/U

6. What happens to the molecules in a gas when the temperature is decreased? (12.2) K/U

7. Complete the graphic organizer below, demonstrating how Boyle's law and Charles' law contribute to the ideal gas law. Also demonstrate how the ideal gas law contributes to the combined gas law. (12.2) C A

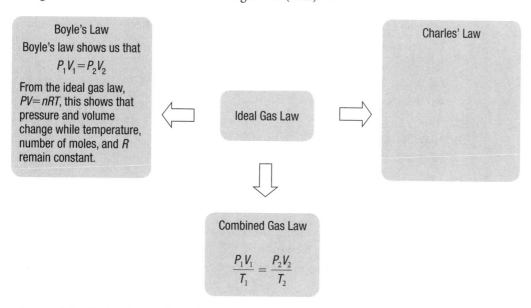

Boyle's Law

Boyle's law shows us that

$$P_1V_1 = P_2V_2$$

From the ideal gas law, $PV=nRT$, this shows that pressure and volume change while temperature, number of moles, and R remain constant.

Ideal Gas Law

Charles' Law

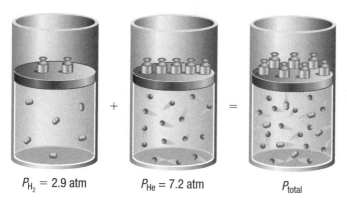

Combined Gas Law

$$\frac{P_1V_1}{T_1} = \frac{P_2V_2}{T_2}$$

8. Applying Dalton's law of partial pressures, what is the total pressure in **Figure 1**? (12.4) T/I

$P_{H_2} = 2.9$ atm $P_{He} = 7.2$ atm P_{total}

Figure 1 Partial pressure and total pressure

1. Which of the following is *not* a form of motion for matter? (11.1) K/U
   (a) translational
   (b) vibrational
   (c) rotational
   (d) horizontal

2. The _____ is a dry region that contains a slightly higher than normal concentration of ozone. (11.2) K/U
   (a) stratosphere
   (b) thermosphere
   (c) mesosphere
   (d) troposphere

3. Is each of the following statements true or false? If you think the statement is false, rewrite it to make it true. K/U
   (a) The Air Quality Health Index is used to identify acids and bases. (11.4)

   (b) Off-gassing occurs when volatile organic compounds are released from materials at room temperature. (12.5)

4. If the temperature and pressure of a gas are held constant in a balloon, how can the volume of the gas be increased? (12.1) T/I

5. Describe what happens to the molecules of a gas if its temperature is decreased. (12.2) T/I

6. Fill in **Table 1** to differentiate between standard temperature and pressure, and ambient temperature and pressure. (11.7) K/U

Table 1 Differences Between Standard and Ambient Temperature and Pressure

	Standard	Ambient
temperature		
pressure		

7. Complete the graphic organizer below, describing the properties of gases at normal pressure and temperature, at high pressure, and at low temperature. (12.2) K/U C A

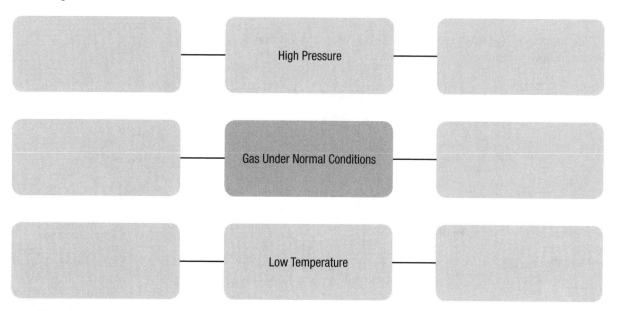

8. The apparatus seen in **Figure 2** is commonly used for collecting a gas over water (12.4) K/U T/I

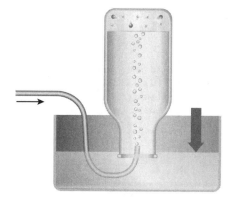

Figure 2

(a) What happens when gas is bubbled into the water?

(b) When all of the water is pushed out of the container, what will remain?

(c) If you measured the total pressure of the container and found it to be 34 kPa at 25 °C, how could you determine the partial pressure of the gas?

Answers

These pages include numerical and short answers to chapter section questions, chapter questions, and unit questions.

Unit 1

1.1, pp. 2–3
1. mass; space
3. a

1.2, pp. 4–6
5. (a) 8 protons, 8 electrons, 6 neutrons
   (b) 16 protons, 16 electrons, 15 neutrons
   (c) 45 protons, 45 electrons, 18 neutrons
6. (a) 10 protons, 4 neutrons, 10 electrons
   7 protons, 7 neutrons, 7 electrons

1.3, pp. 7–9
1. 2, 8
2. d
3. F
6. (b) sulfide
7. (a) cupric, copper(II)
   (b) chloride
   (c) plumbous, lead(II)
   (d) sulfite
8. stannous
9. ferric oxide

1.4, pp. 10–12
1. protons; neutrons
2. T
3. (c) C-12
   (d) N-14
   (e) N-15
   (f) C-14
8. 65.5 u

1.5, pp. 13–14
1. groups; valence electrons
2. F
3. a
8. calcium

1.6, p. 15
1. John Newlands
2. F
3. c

1.7, pp. 16–18
1. b
2. c
3. half; nuclei
7. released
8. a

Chapter 1 Questions, pp. 20–21
1. (a) empirical
   (b) empirical
   (c) theoretical
   (d) theoretical
2. b

3. F
4. (a) 7 u
   (b) 1.162×10^{-26} kg
8. arsenic

2.1, pp. 22–23
1. metal; non-metal
2. electrostatic
3. a
4. T

2.2, pp. 24–26
1. F
2. a
3. non-metal
4. low; low
7. b

2.3, pp. 27–28
1. F
2. right
3. a
5. c

2.4, pp. 29–30
1. two
2. F
3. b
4. +5
5. (a) Ca_3N_2
   (b) $Mg(NO_3)_2$
6. (a) calcium fluoride
   (b) aluminum oxide
   (c) sodium sulfide
   (d) zinc iodide
7. lead(II) phosphate
8. (a) copper(II) chloride
   (b) iron(II) bromide
   (c) iron(III) chloride
   (d) lead(IV) bromide
9. (a) dinitrogen pentoxide
   (b) copper(II) fluoride
   (c) aluminum nitrate

2.5, p. 31
1. energy
2. F
3. a

Chapter 2 Questions, pp. 33–34
1. F
2. c
7. −4
8. (a) potassium sulfide
   (b) mercury(II) phosphate
9. (a) $ZnCrO_4$
   (b) $PbBr_2$

3.1, pp. 35–36
1. living things; fossil fuels
2. T
4. c

3.2, p. 37
1. repellent; insecticide
3. d

3.3, pp. 38–40
1. electronegative
2. T
3. b
5. polar
6. non-polar
7. polar
8. non-polar
9. polar

3.4, pp. 41–42
1. ionic bonds; intermolecular
2. F
3. d
4. van der Waals
6. (b) dipole-dipole force
7. (a) 0
   (b) non-polar

3.5, pp. 43–44
1. T
2. b
3. (i) solid state or liquid state
   (ii) solid state, liquid state, or gas state
   (iii) solid state only

3.6, pp. 45–46
1. T
3. (a) ii, iii
   (b) i, ii
4. b
6. 3, 4, 6, 1, 7, 5, 2

Chapter 3 Questions, pp. 48–49
1. d
2. (a) F
   (b) F
6. (a) 1, 5
   (b) 5, 4
   (c) 1, 3
   (d) 5, 3
   (e) 1, 3
   (f) 1, 4

Unit 1 Questions, pp. 50–51
1. a
3. F
5. (a) zinc bromide
   (b) lead(IV) phosphide
6. (a) Li_2O
   (b) Cu_3N_2
8. (a) not special
   (b) special
   (c) special
   (d) not special
   (e) special

(f) special
(g) special

Unit 2

4.1, pp. 53–54
5. (a) no
6. precipitate
8. the law of conservation of mass
11. (a) $CH_4(g) + 2 O_2(g) \rightarrow CO_2(g) + 2 H_2O(l)$
    (b) $2 Mg(s) + O_2(g) \rightarrow 2 MgO(s)$
    (c) $2 Fe(s) + 3 Cl_2(g) \rightarrow 2 FeCl_3(aq)$
    (d) $2 C_2H_6(g) + 7 O_2(g) \rightarrow 4 CO_2(g) + 6 H_2O(l)$

4.2, pp. 55–57
1. b
5. F
6. atoms
9. d
10. T

4.3, p. 58
2. decomposition
3. (a) synthesis
   (b) $H_2(g) + CO(g) \rightarrow CH_3OH(g)$
   (c) $2 H_2(g) + CO(g) \rightarrow CH_3OH(g)$

4.4, pp. 59–61
2. (b) precipitate
5. F
8. a
10. (a) $Cl_2(aq) + 2 NaBr(aq) \rightarrow Br_2(aq) + 2 NaCl(aq)$
    (b) $Br_2(g) + 2 KI(s) \rightarrow 2 KBr(s) + I_2(g)$
    (c) no reaction

4.6, pp. 63–64
1. c
2. F
8. $H_2CO_3(aq) \rightarrow H_2O(l) + CO_2(g)$
10. (a) $HCl(l) + NaOH(aq) \rightarrow NaCl(s) + H_2O(l)$
    (b) $H_2SO_4(l) + 2 NH_4OH(l) \rightarrow (NH_4)_2SO_4(l) + 2 H_2O(l)$
    (c) $2 NaOH(aq) + H_2CO_3(l) \rightarrow Na_2CO_3(aq) + 2 H_2O(l)$

Chapter 4 Questions, pp. 66–67
1. d
2. a
3. (a) T
   (b) F

5.1, pp. 68–70
1. T
2. thermal energy; light

3. carbon dioxide; carbon monoxide; water
5. a
6. a
8. F
14. C(s)
15. (a) $C_8H_{18} + O_2(g) \rightarrow$
$\quad\quad\quad\quad C(s) + H_2O(l)$
$\quad C_8H_{18} + O_2(g) \rightarrow$
$\quad\quad\quad\quad CO(g) + H_2O(l)$
(b) $2 C_8H_{18} + 9 O_2(g) \rightarrow$
$\quad\quad 16 C(s) + 18 H_2O(l)$
$\quad 2 C_8H_{18} + 17 O_2(g) \rightarrow$
$\quad\quad 16 CO(g) + 18 H_2O(l)$
(c) $C_8H_{18} + O_2(g) \rightarrow$
$\quad\quad\quad CO_2(g) + H_2O(l)$
$\quad 2 C_8H_{18} + 25 O_2(g) \rightarrow$
$\quad\quad 16 CO_2(g) + 18 H_2O(l)$

5.3, pp. 72–74
2. F
4. (a) hydrogen ions
(c) $HCl(aq) \rightarrow$
$\quad\quad H^+(aq) + Cl^-(aq)$
(d) hydroxide ions
(f) $NaOH(s)$
$\quad\quad \rightarrow Na^+(aq) + OH^-(aq)$
5. (a) hydrogen
6. T
8. (b) $CO_2(g) + H_2O(l) \rightarrow$
$\quad\quad\quad\quad H_2CO_3(aq)$
$\quad H_2CO_3(aq) \rightarrow H^+(aq) +$
$\quad\quad\quad\quad HCO_3^-(aq)$
(c) iv
9. (a) T
(b) $N_2(g) + O_2(g) \rightarrow 2 NO$
(c) $2 NO(g) + O_2(g) \rightarrow$
$\quad\quad\quad\quad 2 NO_2(g)$
(d) $2 NO_2(g) + H_2O(l) \rightarrow$
$\quad\quad HNO_3(aq) + HNO_2(aq)$
(e) $2 NO_2(g) \rightarrow$
$\quad\quad\quad N_2(g) + 2 O_2(g)$

5.4, pp. 75–76
2. (a) Colour A is magenta;
$\quad\quad$ Colour B is clear
(b) 7
7. (b) catalysts

5.5, pp. 77–79
1. mineral
2. surface mining; underground mining
6. smelting
9. (a) bases

5.6, pp. 80–81
1. (b) remediation; total cleanup

5.7, pp. 82–83
2. F
5. c
8. T

Chapter 5 Questions, pp. 85–86
1. c
2. c

3. (a) F
(b) F
4. combustion
5. neutralization reaction

Unit 2 Questions, pp. 87–88
1. b
2. d
3. F
4. c
5. mining
6. (a) no
7. (a) basic
(b) acidic

Unit 3

6.1, pp. 90–91
1. F
2. c
5. c
6. (a) quantitative
(b) qualitative
(c) quantitative

6.2, p. 92
1. F
2. 3, 1, 5, 6, 7, 2, 4

6.3, pp. 93–95
1. dividing; a single entity
2. T
3. c
5. 506 nails
8. F
9. (a) greater than
(b) less than
(c) less than
(d) equal to
(e) less than
(f) less than
10. d
11. (a) vi
(b) vii
(c) v
(d) ii
(e) iii
(f) iv
(g) i
12. (a) 2×10^4
(b) 5.798×10^1
(c) 6.0×10^{-2}

6.4, pp. 96–98
1. F
2. 48.55 u
3. a
4. (a) 64.07 g/mol
(b) 46.08 g/mol
5. (a) 110.98 g/mol
(b) 241.88 g/mol
7. b
8. 0.806 mol
9. 0.852 mol

6.5, pp. 99–101
1. N_A, Avogadro's constant
3. d
5. 1.785×10^{24} atoms
6. 5.87×10^{24} molecules

7. (a) 3.1×10^{22} molecules
(b) 6.2×10^{22} atoms
$\quad 3.1 \times 10^{22}$ atoms
$\quad 1.2 \times 10^{23}$ atoms

6.6, pp. 102–104
1. water, carbon dioxide
2. c
3. T
6. 29.06 % O, 5.51 % H, 65.43 % C
7. 44.87 % K, 18.40 % S, 36.72 % O

6.7, pp. 105–106
1. a
2. F
3. d
5. Cu_3P_2
6. H_2SiO_3

6.8, p. 107
2. F
4. a

6.9, pp. 108–109
1. natural; carbon; hydrogen
2. F
4. b
6. $C_5H_{10}O_5$
7. $C_4H_{10}O_2$

Chapter 6 Questions, pp. 111–112
1. (a) quantitative
(b) qualitative
2. F
5. (a) the silver nugget
(b) 1.06×10^{23} more atoms
8. $C_7H_6O_3$

7.1, pp. 113–114
1. 3 : 2
2. F
3. c
5. 6.50 mol
6. 3.8×10^{-1} mol

7.2, pp. 115–116
1. mass; molar mass
2. 2 moles; 1 mole
3. T
5. 63.05 g
6. 124.0 g

7.3, pp. 117–118
1. F
2. d
3. (b) 150 mL
(c) 10 mL
(d) 20 mL
4. a
6. (a) incomplete combustion
(b) complete combustion

7.4, pp. 119–120
1. A
2. A
3. d
4. (a) Y and Z
(b) X and Z
(c) Z

5. 330 g
6. (b) 2 moles
7. 29.7 g

7.5, pp. 121–123
1. actual, theoretical
2. T
3. (a) 80 %
(b) 105 %
5. 42 %
6. 92.84 %
7. 75.26 %

Chapter 7 Questions, pp. 125–126
1. (a) $P_4(s) + 5 O_2(g) \rightarrow 2 P_2O_5(g)$
(b) 5:2
(c) 0.5 moles
2. (a) F
(b) T
3. b
4. 33.41 g
5. (a) $2 X_2 + 3 Y \rightarrow X_4Y_3$
6. (a) chlorine
(b) 220.3 g
(c) 80.06 %

Unit 3 Questions, pp. 127–128
2. c
3. F
6. 129.3 g
8. 69.2 g
9. (a) chlorine
(b) 266.6 g
(c) 21.9 %

Unit 4

8.1, pp. 130–132
5. a
6. polarity
8. (a) ii
(b) iv
(c) iii
(d) i
14. a

8.2, pp. 133–134
1. a
4. solvent
5. (a) F
(b) T
7. concentration

8.3, pp. 135–136
1. b
2. $NaOH(s) \rightarrow Na^+(aq) +$
$\quad\quad\quad\quad OH^-(aq)$
3. (a) F
(b) F
6. (a) yes
(b) polar solvent
(c) non-polar solute
7. soaps; detergents
8. fats; oils; base

8.5, pp. 138–139
1. c
2. supersaturated
3. F

4. (a) 20 g
   (c) unsaturated
7. cool; warm

8.6, pp. 140–141
1. b
6. b
7. 0.035 mol/L

8.7, pp. 142–143
1. b
3. F
5. c
6. 10.0 mL

8.8, pp. 144–145
1. c = quantity of solute ÷ quantity of solution
2. 30 %
3. 1 g/mL at 20° C
5. a
6. 10 L
7. weight
9. 3.4 % W/V

Chapter 8 Questions, pp. 147–148
1. b
2. (a) F
   (b) F
   (c) F
7. (a) 20 g glucose/100 g H_2O
   (d) 15 g glucose

9.1, pp. 149–151
1. (i) formula equations
   (ii) total ionic equations
   (iii) net ionic equations
3. (a) aqueous
   (b) solid
   (c) aqueous
   (d) aqueous
4. a
6. F
7. $3 Ca^{2+}(aq) + 6 Cl^-(aq) + 6 K^+(aq) + 2 PO_4^{3-}(aq) \rightarrow Ca_3(PO_4)_2(s) + 6 K^+(aq) + 6 Cl^-(aq)$
310. net ionic
11. (a) total ionic equation:
    $Ba^{2+}(aq) + SO_4^{2-}(aq) + 2 K^+(aq) + S^{2-}(aq) \rightarrow BaS(s) + 2 K^+(aq) + SO_4^{2-}(aq)$
    net ionic equation:
    $Ba^{2+}(aq) + S^{2-}(aq) \rightarrow BaS(s)$
    (b) SO_4^{2-} (aq) and 2 K$^+$(aq)

9.2, pp. 152–153
3. leachate
4. F
6. c

9.3, p. 154
2. (a) both
   (b) quantitative

(c) qualitative
(d) quantitative
4. filtrate
6. F

9.5, pp. 156–157
2. a
5. F
6. 0.050 L
7. $BaCl_2(s) \rightarrow Ba^{2+}(aq) + 2 Cl^-(aq)$
9. c
10. 0.215 mol/L lead ions, 0.143 mol/L phosphate ions

Chapter 9 Questions, pp. 159–160
1. a
2. F
3. formula
4. no; $Pb(OH)_2 + 2 HCl \rightarrow PbCl_2 + 2 H_2O$
5. (a) total ionic equation:
    $Ca^{2+}(aq) + CO_3^{2-}(aq) + Ba^{2+}(aq) + 2 Cl^-(aq) \rightarrow Ca^{2+}(aq) + 2 Cl^-(aq) + BaCO_3(s)$
    net ionic equation:
    $CO_3^{2-}(aq) + Ba^{2+}(aq) \rightarrow BaCO_3(s)$
    (b) $Ca^{2+}(aq)$ and 2 Cl$^-$(aq)
8. $KCl(s) \rightarrow K^+(aq) + Cl^-(aq)$

10.1, pp. 161–162
2. b
3. demineralization
6. hydrogen gas; compounds of the metal
7. F
9. (a) base
   (b) acid
   (c) acid
10. (a) chlorous acid
    (b) ClO_2^-, chlorite ion

10.2, pp. 163–164
2. dissociation
3. $H^+(aq) + OH^-(aq) \rightarrow H_2O(l)$
4. ionization
6. F
8. one

10.3, pp. 165–166
1. T
3. F
7. (a) base
8. 25 mL titrant
9. primary standard
10. 0.0241 mol/L

Chapter 10 Questions, pp. 168–169
1. strong
2. F
4. (a) hydrochloric acid
   (b) hydrosulfuric acid
   (c) HF

6. dissociate
9. standard
11. 0.0150 mol/L

Unit 4 Questions, pp. 170–171
1. a
2. a
3. F
5. $KCl(s) \rightarrow K^+(aq) + Cl^-(aq)$
7. 0.53 mol/L
9. $Ag(s) + CuCl_2(aq) \rightarrow$ no reaction
11. phosphoric acid

Unit 5

11.1, pp. 173–175
5. b
7. F
10. c
11. a change in state

11.2, pp. 176–178
1. b
2. F
4. d
8. nitrogen
12. T

11.3, p. 179
2. (a) e.g., He, Ne

11.4, pp. 180–181
2. particulate matter
6. incomplete
7. F

11.5, pp. 182–183
1. (i) printers and copiers in home offices
   (ii) combustion in fireplaces
   (iii) lit candles and cigarettes
2. off-gassing
3. F
8. $2 CH_4(g) + 3 O_2(g) \rightarrow 2 CO(g) + 4 H_2O(l)$
9. radon
11. high

11.7, pp. 185–186
1. b
2. F
4. (a) 101 kPa
   (b) atmospheres
6. 665 mm Hg
8. F

11.8, pp. 187–188
1. −273.15
2. F
3. 323 K
7. 0.45 L

11.9, pp. 189–191
1. decreases
2. a
3. F

5. 0.14 kPa
7. c
8. F
9. kinetic
10. 1.2 Pa
11. c
12. 250 °C

Chapter 11 Questions, pp. 193–194
1. b
2. d
3. (a) F
   (b) T
4. stratosphere; mesosphere; thermosphere
8. (a) Boyle's law

12.1, pp. 195–197
1. b
3. mole; volume
6. 0.700 g
7. F
8. a

12.2, pp. 198–200
1. T
4. 310 kPa
6. c
7. F

12.4, pp. 202–203
1. b
2. F
6. 16 kPa
7. (a) increase
8. 62.8 kPa

12.5, pp. 204–205
1. a
2. F
3. b
4. (a) $2 C_8H_{18}(g) + 25 O_2(g) \rightarrow 16 CO_2(g) + 18 H_2O(g)$
   (b) 1500 mL
5. F
6. 80 L

12.6, p. 206
1. F

Chapter 12 Questions, pp. 208–209
1. b
2. d
3. (a) F
   (b) F
4. ideal
8. 10.1 kPa

Unit 5 Questions, pp. 210–211
1. d
2. a
3. (a) F
   (b) T

Appendix

A-1 Taking Notes: Identifying the Main Ideas

- *Identify and highlight the main ideas.* Main ideas are key concepts within a text. Text features such as headings, subheadings, boldfaced or italicized words, and graphic clues help to identify the main ideas in a text.
- *Identify and underline the details.* Details clarify or elaborate on the main ideas within a text.
- When you study for an exam, focus on the main ideas, not the details.

EXAMPLE

Pure Substances

All matter can be classified as pure substances or mixtures. A **pure substance** is matter that contains only one type of particle. For example, copper wire is made from only copper particles. Water is a pure substance that contains only water particles. A **mixture** contains two or more pure substances, such as table salt dissolved in water, or iron mixed with sulfur.

Pure substances can be further classified as elements or compounds. Elements are the basic building blocks of matter. An **element** is a pure substance that cannot be changed into anything simpler. An element contains only one kind of particle. By 1000 BCE, the physical properties of some of the metal elements (such as copper, zinc, silver, and gold) were understood, but none of these were recognized yet as elements. Today, we know that there are at least 116 elements.

Description/Discussion of Strategies

Read the sample text above and note the text features. Remember that text features such as headings and boldfaced words signal key concepts. Notice that the above text has the heading "Pure Substances." The heading is a text feature that tells you the topic of the text. It gives you important information and is, therefore, a key concept. Highlight the heading. Now look at the boldfaced words in the text: **pure substances**, **mixture**, and **element**. Boldfaced words identify vocabulary terms. Here, the boldfaced words are embedded in vocabulary definitions and tell you what the words mean. Highlight vocabulary definitions as they are key concepts, too. Finally, take a look at the opening sentences in both paragraphs of the above text. The opening sentences give you a quick overview of the information in the two paragraphs and should also be highlighted as key concepts.

Now that you have identified the main ideas in the above text, try to find the details. Look for sentences that add to the main ideas you identified above. The sentence "For example, copper wire is made from only copper particles" is an illustration of the sentence "A **pure substance** is matter that contains only one type of particle." It is a detail and should be underlined. Similarly, the last three sentences in the text are also details because they tell more about elements, the main idea. Underline the three sentences.

Read the following text and complete the activities below.

Distinguishing between Empirical Formula and Molecular Formula

CH_2O is an example of an empirical formula. The **empirical formula** gives the simplest whole-number ratio of atoms or ions in a compound. Both methanal and ethanoic acid have the same empirical formula: CH_2O. A **molecular formula** gives the exact number of each type of atom in a compound. A methanal molecule contains 1 carbon atom, 2 hydrogen atoms, and 1 oxygen atom. Therefore, its empirical and molecular formulas are identical. However, an ethanoic acid molecule contains twice the number of atoms given in its empirical formula. As a result, its molecular formula is $C_2H_4O_2$.

1. Highlight the main ideas in the text.
2. Underline the details in the text.

Now read the following text and answer the questions that follow.

There are no intermolecular forces in ionic compounds because ionic compounds do not contain molecules. Ionic compounds are always solids at room temperature. In an ionic crystal, ionic bonds hold all the ions together. There is no difference between the bonds that hold together one formula unit of the compound and those that hold all of the formula units together in a crystal.

　　Ionic bonds are, in general, very strong. This accounts for the high melting point of ionic compounds. Sodium chloride, for example, must be heated to 801 °C before it will become a liquid.

1. Which sentence from the text does *not* contain a main idea?
   (a) There are no intermolecular forces in ionic compounds because ionic compounds do not contain molecules.
   (b) Sodium chloride, for example, must be heated to 801 °C before it will become a liquid.
   (c) In an ionic crystal, ionic bonds hold all the ions together.
   (d) Ionic bonds are, in general, very strong.
2. Explain the difference between a main idea and a detail.

A-1 Taking Notes: Reading Strategies

The skills and strategies that you use to help you read depend on the type of material you are reading. Reading a science book is different from reading a novel. When you are reading a science book, you are reading for information.

BEFORE READING

Skim the section you are going to read. Look at the illustrations, headings, and subheadings.
- *Preview.* What is this section about? How is it organized?
- *Make connections.* What do I already know about the topic? How is it connected to other topics I already know about?

- *Predict.* What information will I find in this section? Which parts provide the most information?
- *Set a purpose.* What questions do I have about the topic?

DURING READING

Pause and think as you read. Spend time on the photographs, illustrations, tables, and graphs, as well as on the words.

- *Check your understanding.* What are the main ideas in this section? How would I state them in my own words? What questions do I still have? Should I reread? Do I need to read more slowly, or can I read more quickly?
- *Determine the meanings of key science terms.* Can I figure out the meanings of terms from context clues in the words or illustrations? Do I understand the definitions in bold type? Is there something about the structure of a new term that will help me remember its meaning? Which terms should I look up in the glossary?
- *Make inferences.* What conclusions can I make from what I am reading? Can I make any conclusions by "reading between the lines"?
- *Visualize.* What mental pictures can I make to help me understand and remember what I am reading? Should I make a sketch?
- *Make connections.* How is the information in this section like information I already know?
- *Interpret visuals and graphics.* What additional information can I get from the photographs, illustrations, tables, or graphs?

AFTER READING

Many of the strategies you use during reading can also be used after reading. For example, your textbook provides summaries and questions at the ends of sections. These questions will help you check your understanding and make connections to information you have just read or to other parts in the textbook.

At the end of each chapter are summary questions and a vocabulary list, followed by a Chapter Self-Quiz and Chapter Review.

- *Locate needed information.* Where can I find the information I need to answer the questions? Under what heading might I find the information? What terms in bold type should I look for? What details do I need to include in my answers?
- *Synthesize.* How can I organize the information? What graphic organizer could I use? What headings or categories could I use?
- *React.* What are my opinions about this information? How does it, or might it, affect my life or my community? Do other students agree with my reactions? Why or why not?

- *Evaluate information.* What do I know now that I did not know before? Have any of my ideas changed because of what I have read? What questions do I still have?

A-1 Taking Notes: Graphic Organizers

Graphic organizers are diagrams that are used to organize and display ideas visually. Graphic organizers are especially useful in science and technology studies when you are trying to connect together different concepts, ideas, and data. Different organizers have different purposes. They can be used to

- show processes
- organize ideas and thinking
- compare and contrast
- show properties of characteristics
- review words and terms
- collaborate and share ideas

TO SHOW PROCESSES

Graphic organizers can show the stages in a process (**Figure 1**).

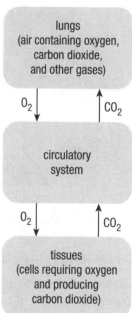

Figure 1 This graphic organizer shows that oxygen and carbon dioxide are transported around the body

TO ORGANIZE IDEAS AND THINKING

A **concept map** is a diagram showing the relationships between ideas (**Figure 2**). Words or pictures representing ideas are connected by arrows and words or expressions that explain the connections. You can use a concept map to brainstorm what you already know, to map your thinking, or to summarize what you have learned.

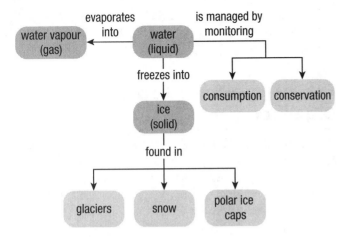

Figure 2 Concept maps show the relationships among ideas

Mind maps are similar to concept maps, but they do not have explanations for the connections between ideas.

You can use a **tree diagram** to show concepts that can be broken down into smaller categories (**Figure 3**).

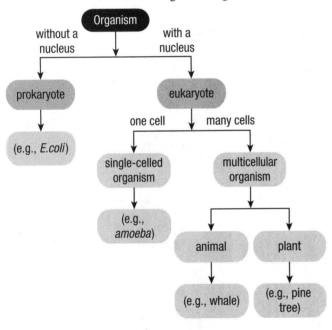

Figure 3 Tree diagrams are very useful for classification

You can use a **fishbone diagram** to organize the important ideas under the major concepts of a topic that you are studying (**Figure 4**).

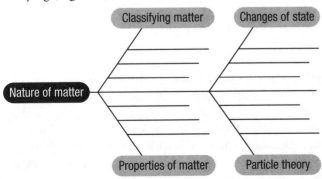

Figure 4 A fishbone diagram

You can use a **K-W-L** chart to write down what you know (K), what you want (W) to find out, and, afterwards, what you have learned (L) (**Figure 5**).

K	W	L
What I know	What I want to know	What I have learned

Figure 5 A K-W-L chart

TO COMPARE AND CONTRAST

You can use a **comparison matrix** (a type of table) to compare related concepts (**Table 1**).

Table 1 Subatomic Particles

	Proton	Neutron	Electron
electrical charge	positive	neutral	negative
symbol	p+	n^0	e^-
location	nucleus	nucleus	orbit around the nucleus

You can use a **Venn diagram** to show similarities and differences (**Figure 6**).

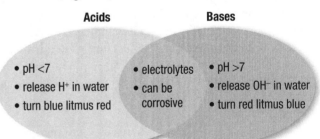

Figure 6 A Venn diagram

You can use a **compare-and-contrast chart** to show similarities and differences between two substances, actions, ideas, and so on (**Figure 7**).

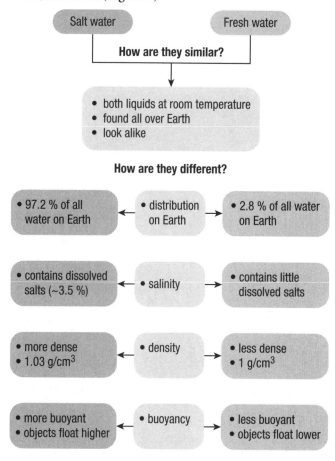

Figure 7 A compare-and-contrast chart

TO SHOW PROPERTIES OR CHARACTERISTICS

You can use a **bubble map** to show properties or characteristics (**Figure 8**).

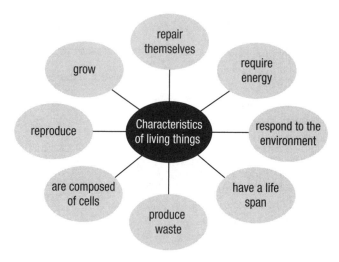

Figure 8 A bubble map

TO REVIEW WORDS AND TERMS

You use a **word wall** to list, in no particular order, the key words and concepts for a topic (**Figure 9**).

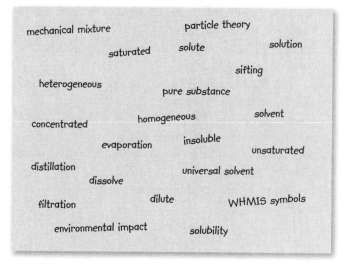

Figure 9 A word wall

TO COLLABORATE AND SHARE IDEAS

When you are working in a small group, you can use a **placemat organizer** to write down what you know about a certain topic. Then all group members discuss their answers and write in the middle section what you have in common (**Figure 10**).

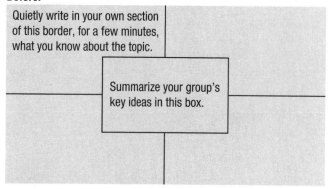

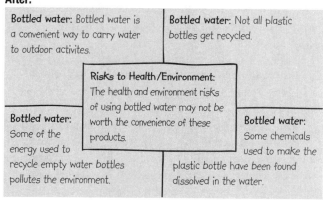

Figure 10 A placemat organizer

A-2 Answering Questions:
Multiple-Choice Questions

- Read the question stem and attempt to answer it before looking at the answer choices.
- Analyze the key words or phrases that tell you what the question stem is asking.
- Read all the answer choices and choose one that most closely matches your answer.
- If your answer is not among the answer choices, reread the question stem. Sometimes slowing your reading pace can help you better understand the meaning of the question.
- Cross out any answer choices that you know are incorrect.

EXAMPLE

Read the following question stem:

Which layer of the Sun is outward from the convective zone and is also not a solid surface?

Description/Discussion of Strategies

Try to answer the question first without looking at the answer options (cover the options with a sheet of paper or with your hand). Then, look at the answer options below. Check your answer against the four choices given. Is your answer among the options? If yes, you have correctly answered the question.

(a) corona

(b) photosphere

(c) radiative zone

(d) solar prominences

If your answer does not match one of the options, use the next strategy. Note the key words in italics in the sample question. The key words and phrases are the essence of the question. They tell you what the question is expecting you to know or do. This sample question asks you to recognize a "layer" of the Sun that is "outward from the convective zone."

Look at the answer options. Which of them is a layer of the Sun? Are there any answer options that you know are wrong? You probably know that the corona and the radiative zone are not *outward from the convective zone*, so you can eliminate answer choices (a) and (c).

You have narrowed your possible answers to B and D, which are both outward from the convective zone. However, are these two *layers* of the Sun? Solar prominences are part of the photosphere, but they are not a layer of the Sun. Therefore, you can eliminate answer choice (d). You are left with option (b), which is the correct answer.

Complete the following multiple-choice questions using the tips you just read.

1. Which of the following is an example of a theory?

   (a) The gravity of Earth pulls objects toward its surface.

   (b) An atom is made up of smaller particles called protons, neutrons, and electrons.

   (c) For every action, there is an equal and opposite reaction.

   (d) Mass is not created or destroyed in normal changes.

   Explain how you arrived at the answer to the above question.

2. Which of the following terms refers to using living things to remove pollutants from a contaminated site?

   (a) bioremediation

   (b) electrolysis

   (c) solidification

   (d) oxidation

   Were there any key words or phrases within the stem that identified what the question is expecting you to know? Explain.

3. Which of the following is an example of a green solvent?

   (a) alcohol

   (b) biodegradable plastic

   (c) recycled fleece

   (d) water

   Which answer choices were you able to eliminate and why?

A-2 Answering Questions: Short-Answer/Written-Response Questions

A **short-answer question** is an open-ended question that requires a response. The question could ask for a definition, an explanation, or an example. It could also be a calculation or a completion activity. Depending on the type of short-answer question, the response will vary in length from a single sentence to a few sentences.

- Read the question carefully to understand the type of response required.
- Organize your response before writing it by making an outline, listing main points, drawing a sketch, or creating a graphic organizer.
- Make sure you answer all parts of the question. Eliminate any unnecessary information from your answer so it is clear and concise.

Read the following selection and answer the short-answer question:

The Phases of the Moon

During the new moon phase, the Moon is not visible from Earth (except during a solar eclipse). We do not see the new moon because the side that is illuminated by the Sun is not facing us. After this phase, the positions of Earth and the Moon allow a larger and larger portion of the Moon's illuminated side to be seen from Earth. The Moon is waxing, or appearing to increase in size. The waxing crescent Moon appears like an arched sliver of light.

1. Describe two phases of the lunar cycle.

Description/Discussion of Strategies

Read the question and identify what type of short-answer question it is. This sample question asks you to *describe* two phases of the lunar cycle. In other words, the question requires an answer that is at least a couple of sentences long. Notice that five lines have been provided for you to write your answer. Use this to estimate your answer's length.

Start by writing down the main points that your answer should cover. These notes will help you craft a complete answer. The sample notes below list the main points regarding two phases of the lunar cycle.

SAMPLE STUDENT NOTES:

– *new moon phase is usually not seen from Earth*

– *new moon phase is seen during a solar eclipse*

– *illumination increases after new moon phase*

– *waxing crescent is a curved slice of light*

You will build your answer from these bullet points. After writing an answer, read it to make sure you have answered the question correctly and completely.

Finally, eliminate any information in your answer that is unnecessary or that does not pertain to the question. If your response is very long, condense the information to make it brief and succinct.

SAMPLE ANSWER:

Two phases of the lunar cycle are the new moon phase and the waxing crescent. The new moon phase is usually not seen from Earth because the side of the Moon that faces us is not illuminated. The new moon phase can be seen only during a solar eclipse. Illumination of the Moon increases after the new moon phase. During the waxing crescent phase, the Moon looks like a curved slice of light.

PRACTICE

Complete the following short-answer questions, using the selections below and the tips you just read.

The Issue: The Impact of Agricultural Practices

The current use of fertilizers is not healthy for the environment. Long-term use of fertilizers is known to damage ecosystems, including those that are located some distance from where the fertilizers were applied. On the other hand, the advantage of this agricultural practice is that fertilizers increase crop yields and are cost efficient. However, sustainable agriculture must produce enough crops for the world's increasing population, as well as produce crops without causing permanent damage to the environment. Therefore, the agriculture industry is being challenged to develop and use alternatives that will not interfere with the natural cycling of Earth's matter.

1. What are one advantage and one disadvantage of using fertilizers?

Qualitative and Quantitative Analysis

Qualitative analysis is the identification or detection of a specific substance. Using a urine test strip to detect excess glucose in urine is an example of qualitative analysis. Chemicals at the end of the strip change colour when dipped in urine. A dark colour indicates there is too much glucose in the blood. A paler colour indicates that normal levels of glucose are present. Data collected during this type of analysis are called qualitative data.

The presence of excess glucose in blood can be a sign of diabetes. Diabetics use a device called a glucometer to regularly monitor their blood sugar levels. Typically, a tiny needle pricks the finger to produce a drop of blood. The glucometer absorbs the blood, measures the blood glucose concentration, and reports this value on a digital display. An analysis that provides numerical data is called a **quantitative analysis**.

2. What is the difference between qualitative and quantitative analysis?

What Is a Solution?

A solution is a homogeneous mixture of two or more substances. It is a homogeneous mixture because there is only one phase and the components are uniformly mixed, giving a uniform appearance. As a result, samples taken from two different locations in the solution have exactly the same composition.

Solutions can be solids, liquids, or gases. Liquid and gaseous solutions are transparent because the entities they contain are too small to block light as it passes through. Solutions may be coloured or colourless depending on the substances they contain.

3. Describe the characteristics of a solution.

A-3 The Periodic Table

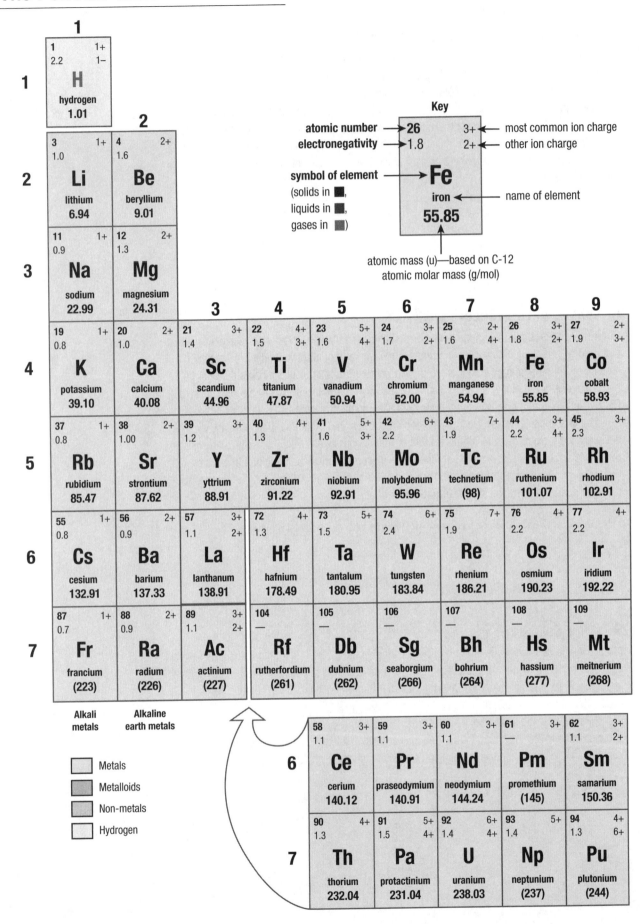

Measured values are subject to change as experimental techniques improve. Atomic molar mass values in this table are based on IUPAC website values (2005 and 2007).

					18
13	14	15	16	17	2 — **He** helium 4.00 **1**

10	11	12						

Group 13–18 upper blocks

5 — 2.0 **B** boron 10.81
6 — 2.6 **C** carbon 12.01
7 3− 3.0 **N** nitrogen 14.01
8 2− 3.4 **O** oxygen 16.00
9 1− 4.0 **F** fluorine 19.00
10 — **Ne** neon 20.18 **2**

13 3+ 1.6 **Al** aluminum 26.98
14 — 1.9 **Si** silicon 28.09
15 3− 2.2 **P** phosphorus 30.97
16 2− 2.6 **S** sulfur 32.07
17 1− 3.2 **Cl** chlorine 35.45
18 — **Ar** argon 39.95 **3**

28 2+ 3+ 1.9 **Ni** nickel 58.69
29 2+ 1+ 1.9 **Cu** copper 63.55
30 2+ 1.7 **Zn** zinc 65.41
31 3+ 1.8 **Ga** gallium 69.72
32 4+ 2.0 **Ge** germanium 72.64
33 3− 2.2 **As** arsenic 74.92
34 2− 2.6 **Se** selenium 78.96
35 1− 3.0 **Br** bromine 79.90
36 — 3.0 **Kr** krypton 83.80 **4**

46 2+ 3+ 2.2 **Pd** palladium 106.42
47 1+ 1.9 **Ag** silver 107.87
48 2+ 1.7 **Cd** cadmium 112.41
49 3+ 1.8 **In** indium 114.82
50 4+ 2+ 2.0 **Sn** tin 118.71
51 3+ 5+ 2.1 **Sb** antimony 121.76
52 2− 2.1 **Te** tellurium 127.60
53 1− 2.7 **I** iodine 126.90
54 — 2.6 **Xe** xenon 131.29 **5**

78 4+ 2+ 2.3 **Pt** platinum 195.08
79 3+ 1+ 2.5 **Au** gold 196.97
80 2+ 1+ 2.0 **Hg** mercury 200.59
81 1+ 3+ 1.6 **Tl** thallium 204.38
82 2+ 4+ 2.3 **Pb** lead 207.2
83 3+ 5+ 2.0 **Bi** bismuth 208.98
84 2+ 4+ 2.0 **Po** polonium (209)
85 1− 2.2 **At** astatine (210)
86 — **Rn** radon (222) **6**

110 — **Ds** darmstadtium (281)
111 — **Rg** roentgenium (272)
112 — **Cn** copernicium (285)
113 — **Uut** ununtrium (284)
114 — **Uuq** ununquadium (289)
115 — **Uup** ununpentium (288)
116 — **Uuh** ununhexium (291)
117 — **Uus** ununseptium
118 — **Uuo** ununoctium (294) **7**

Halogens   Noble gases

63 3+ 2+ — **Eu** europium 151.96
64 3+ 1.2 **Gd** gadolinium 157.25
65 3+ — **Tb** terbium 158.93
66 3+ 1.2 **Dy** dysprosium 162.50
67 3+ 1.2 **Ho** holmium 164.93
68 3+ 1.2 **Er** erbium 167.26
69 3+ 1.3 **Tm** thulium 168.93
70 3+ 2+ — **Yb** ytterbium 173.05
71 2+ 1.3 **Lu** lutetium 174.97 **6**

95 3+ 4+ 1.3 **Am** americium (243)
96 3+ 1.3 **Cm** curium (247)
97 3+ 4+ 1.3 **Bk** berkelium (247)
98 3+ 1.3 **Cf** californium (251)
99 3+ 1.3 **Es** einsteinium (252)
100 3+ 1.3 **Fm** fermium (257)
101 2+ 3+ 1.3 **Md** mendelevium (258)
102 2+ 3+ 1.3 **No** nobelium (259)
103 3+ — **Lr** lawrencium (262) **7**